Burning Vision

ALSO BY MARIE CLEMENTS

Copper Thunderbird

The Edward Curtis Project: A Modern Picture Story
(with Rita Leistner)

Tombs of the Vanishing Indian

The Unnatural and Accidental Women

All available from Talonbooks

BURNING VISION

Marie Clements

Talonbooks

Talonbooks
278 East First Avenue, Vancouver, British Columbia, Canada v5T 1A6
www.talonbooks.com

Seventh printing: April 2014

Typeset in Minion
Printed and bound in Canada on 100% post-consumer recycled paper

Cover design by Adam Swica

Talonbooks gratefully acknowledges the financial support of the Canada Council for the Arts, the Government of Canada through the Canada Book Fund, and the Province of British Columbia through the British Columbia Arts Council and the Book Publishing Tax Credit.

Rights to produce *Burning Vision*, in whole or in part, in any medium by any group, amateur or professional, are retained by the author. Interested persons are requested to apply to her agent: Michael Petrasek, Kensington Literary Representation, 34 St. Andrew Street, Toronto, Ontario, Canada M5T 1K6; tel.: (416) 979-0187; email: kensingtonlit@rogers.com.

The timeline on pages 4–5 is modified from one created by Rumble Productions for the original production of *Burning Vision*.

Library and Archives Canada Cataloguing in Publication

Clements, Marie, 1962–
 Burning vision / Marie Clements.

 A play.
 ISBN 0-88922-472-2

 I. Title.
PS8555.L435B87 2003   C812'.6   C2003-910435-4
PR9199.4.C53B87 2003

In loving memory of my beautiful mother
Because love is long …
Love always, Marie

To my "little boy" Devon,
Just because …
Love always, your mother

I would like to thank Norman Armour, Paula Danckert, and Peter Hinton for their integrity and artistry in working beside me to make *Burning Vision* a "reality." I would also like to thank and acknowledge the continued support and generosity of Playwrights' Workshop Montreal, Rumble Theatre, The Firehall Arts Centre, and The Banff Playwrights Colony.

And to all those who have left their strong spirit, good will, and hard work in this production: George Blondin, Alma and Mike Cholak, Captain Mike Arnfinson, Patricia Salanski, Bertram Arnfinson, Robert Zobatar, Takeo Yamashiro, Hiro Kanagawa, Linda Hoffman, Maiko Bae Yamamoto, Shannon Webb, Cindy Gilday, Peter Blow, Dora Arnfinson, Art Furlong, Moira Keller, Bertram Charles Furlong, Rose Furlong, a dynamic design and production team, this beautiful and brave cast. And Joe.

Burning Vision was first produced by Rumble Productions and premiered at the Firehall Arts Centre in Vancouver, British Columbia, on April 26, 2002, with the following cast:

LITTLE BOY
Nathan Dubois

LABINE BROTHER TWO /
THE MINER / STEVEDORE
Marcus Hondro

KOJI
Hiro Kanagawa

THE WIDOW /
THE JAPANESE GRANDMOTHER
Margo Kane

LABINE BROTHER ONE /
DENE ORE CARRIER / STEVEDORE
Kevin Loring

ROUND ROSE / TOYKO ROSE
Julie Tamako Manning

FAT MAN / CAPTAIN MIKE
Allan Morgan

ROSE
Lisa C. Ravensbergen

THE RADIUM PAINTER
Erin Wells

DENE SEER (Vision and Singing)
George Blondin

Directed by Peter Hinton
Produced by Norman Armour
Dramaturg: Paula Danckert
Stage Manager: David Kerr
Costume Design: Barbara Clayden
Props Design: Erinne Drake
Sound Design: Noah Drew
Technical Director: Ken Hollands
Set Design: Andreas Kahre
Lighting Design: John Webber
Slavey translation: George Blondin
Japanese translation: Hiro Kanagawa

Burning Vision was commissioned by Rumble Theatre and developed in partnership with Playwrights' Workshop Montreal (PWM). The play was developed through residences at Rumble, Playwrights' Workshop, and at the Banff Playwright's Colony. Several workshops of *Burning Vision* have been conducted: a first reading of scenes in June 2000 during Playwrights' Workshop's National Women's Writers' Unit, a dramaturgical workshop in April 2001 with Rumble and PWM in Vancouver, readings in September 2001 at Banff, and a design workshop in January 2002 with Rumble and PWM in Vancouver. Throughout the development process, dramaturgy has been provided by Paula Danckert of Playwrights' Workshop Montreal and direction by Peter Hinton.

CHARACTERS

THE DENE SEER (pronounced "see-er") – A Dene medicine man who sang four seer songs over a long night, in the late 1880s. (*voiceover*)

LITTLE BOY – A beautiful Native boy. Eight to ten years old. The personification of the darkest uranium found at the centre of the earth.

FAT MAN – An American bomb-test dummy manning his house in the late 1940s and '50s. He gets more and more human as the bombs draw closer. Unlikeable in a likeable way. In his forties.

ROUND ROSE – An aged Iva Toguri who works in her father's Japanese souvenir store in Chicago, still waiting for an apology by the U.S. government for her prosecution as "Tokyo Rose" – a propaganda radio personality who aired "zero hour" broadcasts during the Second World War. Her "on air" personality was seen as the exotic Japanese geisha girl by American G.I.s. In reality, she is an almost homely Japanese-American student who went to UCLA and believed herself to be American before and after anything else.

THE WIDOW – An older Dene women who keeps a fire of love for her dead Dene ore-carrier husband.

ROSE – A Métis woman in her twenties who walks between Native and non-Native lines as she works in the North at her father's Hudson's Bay Store. A bread-maker and a dreamer looking for her place.

KOJI – A Japanese fisherman just before the blast of the atomic bomb. His spirit holds on to a cherry branch of hope until he transforms himself to the other side of the world.

THE RADIUM PAINTER – A beautiful American woman who paints radium on watch dials in the 1930s. She is looking for the answers to the glow and death of her life.

CAPTAIN MIKE – For more than thirty years, captain of the *Radium Prince,* a barge that transported uranium used in the atom bomb. Icelandic. Late forties to fifty years old. (*voiceover*)

THE JAPANESE GRANDMOTHER – The slow march of a grandmother's hope for her grandson's survival after the dropping of the bomb. (*double cast)

THE MINER – A white Port Radium miner in the depths of the earth. Late twenties/early thirties. (*double cast)

THE BROTHERS LABINE – The two brother prospectors who discovered uranium at the base of Great Bear Lake in the 1930s. Thirty-ish. (*double cast)

THE TWO STEVEDORES – Native boat pilots who navigated the boats of ore downriver. (*double cast)

DENE ORE CARRIER – The widow's husband who emerges from the fire in her dreams and ultimately joins the long line of Dene ore carriers when she is able to let him go into the next world. (*double cast)

RADIO ANNOUNCERS

LORNE GREENE/VOICE OF DOOM

RADIO ANNOUNCER FOR CBC'S *NATIONAL NEWS BULLETIN* – A voice that so characterized the bad news of the Second World War in Canada that it became known as the "voice of doom."

SLAVEY ANNOUNCERS – Community members who broadcast in the North trying to find and reach out over the air to loved ones who are missing from them. In this case, a call and response from this world to the spirit world.

TOKYO ROSE – A 1940s radio siren that embodied the erotic fantasies of U.S. Army men in the Pacific War of the Second World War. In this case, the radio announcer is Round Rose, an older somewhat bitter version of the myth that broadcasts her view from the back storeroom of her father's store.

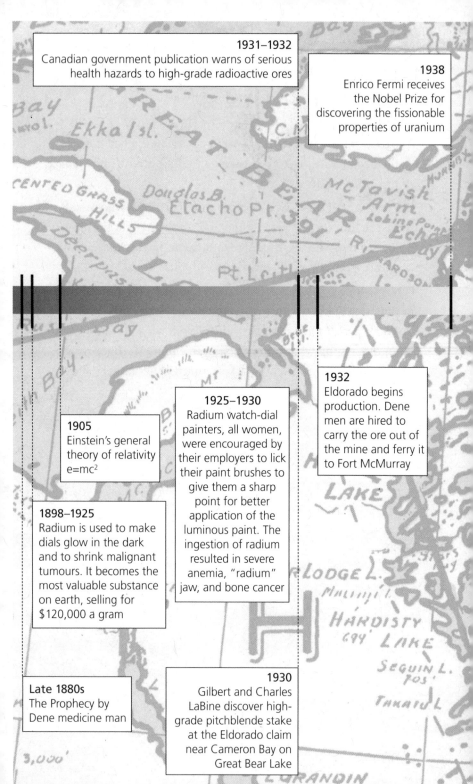

1931–1932
Canadian government publication warns of serious health hazards to high-grade radioactive ores

1938
Enrico Fermi receives the Nobel Prize for discovering the fissionable properties of uranium

1932
Eldorado begins production. Dene men are hired to carry the ore out of the mine and ferry it to Fort McMurray

1925–1930
Radium watch-dial painters, all women, were encouraged by their employers to lick their paint brushes to give them a sharp point for better application of the luminous paint. The ingestion of radium resulted in severe anemia, "radium" jaw, and bone cancer

1905
Einstein's general theory of relativity
$e=mc^2$

1898–1925
Radium is used to make dials glow in the dark and to shrink malignant tumours. It becomes the most valuable substance on earth, selling for $120,000 a gram

1930
Gilbert and Charles LaBine discover high-grade pitchblende stake at the Eldorado claim near Cameron Bay on Great Bear Lake

Late 1880s
The Prophecy by Dene medicine man

1943–1944
Canadian government buys out Eldorado

August 6, 1998
Six Dene residents from Déline travel to Hiroshima to pay respects on the anniversary of the detonation of the atomic bomb

1942
U.S. government orders sixty tons of Port Radium ore

July 16, 1945
The first atomic bomb exploded at the Trinity site, New Mexico

1950
Nevada Test Site established as the on-continent nuclear weapons testing area for U.S. Since this time more than nine hundred atomic explosions have been detonated at this location – sixty-five miles northwest of Las Vegas

1941
Japanese Canadians required to carry identification card with thumbprint and photo

1960
First Dene miner dies of cancer

May 1941
orders eight tons of uranium Eldorado for military research

1948
Iva Toguri arrested in Tokyo, flown to San Francisco, and tried for eight counts of treason as Tokyo Rose

December 7, 1941
Japan attacks Pearl Harbor

August 6, 1945
"Little Boy," first atomic bomb used in warfare, is dropped over Hiroshima, Japan

1942
Japanese-Canadians forced into internment camps; most camps are in BC

1999
Federal government signs commitment to clean up and contain Port Radium mine site

August 9, 1945
Man" is dropped over Nagasaki, Japan

April 26, 2002
Burning Vision opening night

THE FREQUENCY OF DISCOVERY

– Movement One –

Intense darkness is pierced by light that reveals foreboding scenes of human suffering: pain, grief, loss, and isolation.

The sound of loud, strange noises from deep in the earth.

The sound of a radio dial gliding from frequency to frequency, creating different cultural tones and telling different stories. It is as if they are waiting on the radio waves, ready to be heard, and a sense of discovery is heightened.

The sound of an electric switch clicking on and a broadcast that fills the space.

U.S. RADIO ANNOUNCER (*voiceover*)
They are adjusting their goggles. They are in position …
Their high-intensity goggles …

THE COUNTDOWN (*voiceover*)
… 30 seconds.

U.S. RADIO ANNOUNCER (*voiceover*)
  They don't see anything – except we will certainly see the atomic detonation …

THE COUNTDOWN (*voiceover*)
  … 14, 13, 12, 11, 10, 9, 8, 7, 6, 5, 4, 3, 2, 1, 0 …

U.S. RADIO ANNOUNCER (*voiceover*)
  … and the atomic detonation is off and the first impression is …

> *The sound of an explosion that lasts a long time and reaches far into the distance, until at last the explosion is complete and it is quiet. Darkness.*

> *Two flashlight beams pierce the dark.*

> *The sound of radio waves and the static of dead airspace. The sound of the radio dial gliding from station to station. The radio dial stops and tunes in on the sound of two sets of loud footsteps walking over the space.*

> *The two beams of light momentarily flash over the image of a naked Indian boy-man, scared and huddled in the darkness at the centre of the earth.*

LITTLE BOY (*whispering*)
  Every child is scared of the dark, not because it is dark but because they know, sooner or later, they will be discovered. It is only a matter of time …

> *The sound of footsteps and laboured breathing gets closer.*

… before someone discovers you and claims you for themselves. Claims you are you because they found you. Claims you are theirs because they were the first to find you, and lay claims on you …

The sound of footsteps and laboured breathing gets closer and closer. The two beams of light circle toward him.

LITTLE BOY
… Not knowing you've known yourself for thousands of years. Not knowing *you* are not the monster.

The sound of footsteps is close and huge. The laboured breathing is heavy. The two flashlight beams are almost on him. The Indian boy braces himself.

The sound of ROSE's footsteps and then a dull thud.

ROSE
Auhhh! Carry yourself. I'm all tired now.

The two beams of light flash toward the sound and land on a sack of flour lying on the ground. LABINE BROTHER TWO's flashlight momentarily lights ROSE's face.

LABINE BROTHER ONE
Shit, what was that?

LABINE BROTHER TWO
Looks like a sack of something.

LABINE BROTHER ONE
No, really?

LABINE BROTHER TWO
　　I wonder what's in there?

LABINE BROTHER ONE
　　Don't worry your poor brain about what's inside. What
　　you should be worrying about is practical concerns like
　　whose sack is it? Who brought it here? And where are
　　they now?

LABINE BROTHER TWO
　　What do I care?

LABINE BROTHER ONE
　　'Cause it makes perfect sense if a sack is here, somebody
　　else is here. Somebody else might be tryin' to elbow in on
　　our claim, and all you can worry about is, "What's in the
　　sack?" Well, nothing worthwhile is ever just left in a sack.
　　Jesus, do I have to think for both of us at the same time?

　　　　LABINE BROTHER ONE flashes his light across the
　　　　darkness and lands on THE WIDOW, an old Dene
　　　　woman, just as she is about to sit on a log. She reaches
　　　　down and gathers a few small branches together to
　　　　make a fire pile.

　　　　The sound of THE WIDOW striking a match.

LABINE BROTHER TWO
　　What the hell was that?

LABINE BROTHER ONE
　　What?

LABINE BROTHER TWO
　　That sheeek sound. Sounded like a match being struck
　　to me.

LABINE BROTHER ONE
> Relax. Nobody knows about this place except the
> Indians, and they can damn well see in the dark. I'm
> thinking that old Indian we met up with told some other
> prospectors about this place. If he did, I'm gonna ring his
> red neck. You can't trust an Indian with a secret.

LABINE BROTHER TWO
> He didn't exactly say it was a secret. YOU said it was a
> secret. He just said nobody's supposed to go here because
> nobody's supposed to be here. That's all he said. He was
> just being neighbourly and warned us with the story of
> the black rock.

LABINE BROTHER ONE
> Warned us about a black rock! I never been scared of no
> rock. It's dangerous for a prospector to be scared of a
> rock, and it's just plain naive for a grown white man to be
> scared of Indian fairy tales. HERE COMES THE
> BLACK ROCK … Boo! Get a grip before you pee
> your pants.

> *LABINE BROTHER TWO listens carefully.*

LABINE BROTHER TWO
> Shhh … listen … really.

> *LABINE BROTHER TWO shines his light on*
> *THE WIDOW.*

> *As the embers of the fire begin to light up, the sound of*
> *static as a phonograph needle goes round and round*
> *in the tracks of a record. The sound of static begins to*
> *crackle like fire. Long shadows of firelight flicker,*
> *suggesting a man's body rising.*

THE WIDOW (*in part Slavey*)

Hello, you. Hello. I am warming you up to talk to me. It is just you and me sitting by the fire. Yes?

She listens.

You always were the stubborn kind of man never talking unless things were just right. Only talking when you wanted to hear your voice for effect. You made me listen better. I am a real good listener now. You made me learn to hear what you thought in silence. I want you to say one word to me now … just one word … or I will throw your favourite boot in the fire.

She holds it above the fire and listens.

THE WIDOW

See, here it goes. One good rubber boot gonna be melting all over to the other side. Goodbye, boot … good riddance. What?

THE WIDOW and the boot have a serious talk.

You want to say your last rites, boot? Say it now then. There's gotta be a good confession now before you get a rite. What? You walked all over this good woman's floor and left muddy tracks. Well, she is a good, good woman … almost too good for a boot that leaves muddy tracks, but I'm sure you are forgiven. Amen. Here it goes …

She listens.

… Okay … okay I was trying to get a rise from you. Don't worry, I'll put this here boot right beside the other one so you know where it is. See?

LABINE BROTHER ONE

Are you gonna stand there all night, or are we gonna find what we came here to find?

LABINE BROTHER TWO

It's too dark to find anything.

LABINE BROTHER ONE

Well, if you can't see anything then nobody can see you. The trick is you have to be able to feel it in the dark. And if you can't feel it in your bones like a good prospector, we got these flashlights so we can see. We can see what we've come to see and nobody can see what we're seeing. See?

LABINE BROTHER TWO

That's great in principle, Gilbert, but it is really dark here. Black.

LABINE BROTHER ONE

Then it will make our discovery sweeter.

The sound of LABINE BROTHER TWO's stumbling footsteps. The dull sound of his body and flashlight hitting the earth and echoing.

LABINE BROTHER TWO

Ouch … shit …

LABINE BROTHER ONE

Get up, idiot! … Are you all right? Charlie?

LABINE BROTHER ONE lowers his flashlight beam toward his brother.

*The clunk of the needle hitting a record, the start of
a song.*

LABINE BROTHER TWO

Yeah … I'm all right but I broke my light.

*The sound of Hank Williams singing "I Saw the Light"
– a very Canadian rendition – fades in.*

SONG

I wandered so aimless, life filled with sin.
I wouldn't let my dear Saviour in.
Then Jesus came like a stranger in the night.
Praise the Lord, I saw the light.

*The beam from LABINE BROTHER ONE's flashlight
lands on ROSE, and LABINE BROTHER TWO's
flashlight lands on the sack.*

*ROSE, a young Métis woman, lies exhausted beside the
sack of flour on the ground. She begins to talk to it.*

ROSE

Get up, sack, and walk like a man. You, sack, are fat. A
delicate thing like myself shouldn't be carrying a fifty-
pound sack, but that's what happens when you are me.
My mother would say to sing, it will make things lighter.
She had a beautiful voice, my mother; like a canary my
father would say. I've never heard a canary, but I liked
that her voice might be the colour of yellow. It is hard to
be delicate in the North. Here it is better to be practical;
you'll live longer. I'm wearing my mother's Sunday dress
because it is the first day of my new job in my father's
store. Wearing her Sunday dress and carrying this sack of
flour will let him know that I am capable of being a lady

and carrying things that are heavy at the same time. He is worried no one will love a tomboy who can snowshoe better than them, trap better than them, eat better than them. I told him, "I can look after myself. I don't need no bossy husband ..." He gave me the blue eye and said, "Things are different in the old country." My mother would say, "We are the old country." But I don't say nothing. I just listen to my dead mother saying it, and smile at his blue eye ... thinking it. Get up now.

The sound of a fishing line whizzing through space.

LABINE BROTHER TWO
That! That ... I heard that. It went whizzzz ...

LABINE BROTHER ONE
Shut up!

LABINE BROTHER ONE flashes his light toward the whiz and lights the fish.

LABINE BROTHER ONE
It's a goddamn fish. You scared of a fish now?

LABINE BROTHER TWO
When it goes whizz ... I am.

LABINE BROTHER TWO lights the face of the fisherman, KOJI, as he grabs a fish from his line. Holding onto its middle, he brings it closer and talks intimately to it.

KOJI
You, fish, you and me meeting here at the end of a line. Here, let me take you off the hook. The legend about you says there should be one hand on you at all times.

He makes sure the head and tail of the fish are balanced in his grasp and releases the hook from its mouth.

I will put one hand on you, gentle right in the middle, so that the world will not quake when your tail shakes the world's air.

He looks closely at the tail as it shakes back and forth with a controlled flip.

He talks to its head.

You will no longer breathe water and send out the sea through your mouth. You will no longer lie beneath the world.

He brings the fish closer.

KOJI

There will be no tidal waves while I am the fisherman and you are the trout. What did you say? Someone is coming.

ROSE picks up the sack and lifts it to her shoulder. A small hole in the sack begins to stream out a white-flour trail as she walks.

The sound of a record being put on a turntable. The sound of static as the needle goes round and round. Then ...

FAT MAN sits in darkness. His body jolts and he looks up to the sound.

FAT MAN

Did you hear that? No, huh? I hear it.

LABINE BROTHER TWO

Shhh … Did you hear that? I said did you hear that?

*The side lamp goes on in FAT MAN's 1950s living
room. The large sack-dummy of a man sits in his
La-Z-Boy chair, reading a* Playboy *magazine. He
looks intently at his hi-fi radio–TV console across the
distance of his living room.*

FAT MAN

That's what I call high-fidelity sound. To reproduce the
full range of sound heard by the human ear. Hi-fi.

*He then looks around his space. He gets up and begins
to pace.*

FAT MAN

Hi-fi … Hi Fi Fee Fo. I am a part of the world, Daddy-o. I
am part of the world just like this new hi-fi equipment.
Just like this *Playboy,* which states: "A high-fidelity
system is commonly accepted as a badge of sophisticated
masculinity." A badge of sophisticated masculinity
concerned with their environment. Or should I say
lifestyle?

Hi Fi Fee Fo. If I was the interior designer I would've
went with plaid, but hey, a piece of highly trained man
material like myself shouldn't concern themselves with
bare walls. That's for the loonies. I look good. I mean, I'm
dressed for the part and, frankly, between you and me,
that's half the battle.

*He sits back down and gets comfy in his
La-Z-Boy chair.*

If you look the part, people are just as happy to accept that. We want the unreal real thing. We don't want studies. We want tests. We don't want thinking, we want reaction. Highly skilled unthinking reaction. Nice space.

He turns the sidelight out.

ROSE continues to walk in a large circle, the sack streaming a thin white trail behind her that thickens with each round.

LABINE BROTHER TWO sets down his flashlight and the light forms a tunnel.

LABINE BROTHER TWO
I can hear it close now. Can't you?

LABINE BROTHER ONE
I can't hear nothing. Maybe that rock is talking to you.

LABINE BROTHER TWO
And you can't hear anything?

LABINE BROTHER ONE
I don't listen to rocks. I listen to money. Now THAT I can hear. That's what separates one man from another. One man will listen to a rock while one man will listen to money.

LABINE BROTHER TWO
I can hear the rock.

LABINE BROTHER ONE
You can go Indian all you want. But know this. I am going to find that rock, I'm going to stake it, and it will be rightfully mine ... That's how real dreams work.

LABINE BROTHER TWO

If you say so, Gilbert. Discoverin' something big, even if someone told you where it is, is hard on a guy.

The instrumentals of the second verse of "I Saw the Light" come in.

From far away, THE JAPANESE GRANDMOTHER, an old Japanese woman dressed traditionally in a red kimono, carries a heavy burden on her back. She marches in slow motion, steadily, beautifully, toward an outstretched cherry branch. KOJI points to the dream coming through a tunnel of light. He holds the fish tightly as he begins to realize he is watching himself, as a child, being carried by his delicate grandmother.

SONG

Just like a blind man, I wandered along.
Worries and fears I claimed for my own.
Then like the blind man
God gave back my sight.
Praise the Lord, I saw the light.

KOJI stares at THE JAPANESE GRANDMOTHER in amazement as she passes in front of him, carrying his man-body down a long tunnel of light.

KOJI looks into the light.

KOJI

Look, trout … Like a man's dream coming from behind … first a child on his grandmother's back and now the man I am, passing close before me like a faraway dream.

Obachan! What do you think you are doing? Put me down; I am too heavy. Obachan! I am a man and you are an old woman. Obachan! Please … you should be at home resting, not carrying me on your back in a crazy dream. Obachan!

SONG

I saw the light, I saw the light.
No more darkness, no more night.
Now I'm so happy, no sorrow in sight.
Praise the Lord, I saw the light.

The Japanese space takes over as the song ends.

KOJI and the trout slowly follow behind THE JAPANESE GRANDMOTHER as she makes her way down the tunnel …

KOJI

I am riding on my grandmother's back. This is what I see. I am riding on her back yet I am a man. All man legs and tall arms. I am man and yet she is carrying me like I weigh nothing. She is small and delicate, but she walks steadily down hills and up hills at the same pace, ever mindful to keep the steady rhythm that will carry its own will past the pain of burden. I am riding on my grandmother's back, the side of my face, my nose, striking the back of her neck where the bone almost erupts. This same bone coming up through her skin used to keep me company as I used to ride on her back, when I was a child, for long periods of time over long stretches of land.

The sound of a young Japanese boy and his grandmother talking in Japanese. Her laboured breathing as she pauses between steps.

Finally, my grandmother stops and I watch myself slide down her bony landscape. I am to touch the tree and she is to touch my hand and say.

THE JAPANESE GRANDMOTHER takes the man's hand and places it on the tree. She takes her hand and places it over his own as in a vow.

THE JAPANESE GRANDMOTHER

If we ever get separated, wait for me here. Wait for me here and I will come for you. Remember this tree; remember my words:

Wakaretara koko de mattete, ne. Koko de mattetara Obachan ga mukaini kuru kara. Kono ki to Obachan no iutta koto o oboetenasai.

KOJI

Finally, my grandmother nods upward. I watch myself slide up her bony landscape only to be told to stay on this one, this branch. The only tree standing. I climb it. I sit on this one branch.

THE JAPANESE GRANDMOTHER turns and begins to leave. The sound of her soft footsteps walking, echoing off.

I ask, "What does this mean?" She says I will know soon enough. I ask, "Who am I to talk to now?" She says … /

THE JAPANESE GRANDMOTHER stops and turns looking him directly in the eye.

THE JAPANESE GRANDMOTHER

/ I say, you will be safe as long as you talk to the cherry tree's back.

KOJI, startled, drops the trout on the earth.

The tunnel light disappears.

FAT MAN turns on the lamp on his side table.

FAT MAN

I thought I heard something. This hi-fi system is good but it can keep you up at night listening. "Today's listener is a part of the cultural revolution."

He flashes a Time *magazine.*

FAT MAN

I am a part of the cultural revolution, a cultural revolution that hears alien footsteps coming. Shit, but you never hear footsteps far enough away to do anything about them. That's why I'm manning the post. Manning it, get it? I'm an … it and I'm MAN-ing it. What the hell is that anyway? What kind of a job is MAN-ing it? It's a man's job in an unpredictable world. Being an it. Death is predictable in an unpredictable way. I mean, if you knew how it was going to come, you could regret it more. But I guess that's just about like anything in this world. Knowing doesn't stop it from happening. I mean, let's get real, it's just about making yourself feel better in the now. Look at me. I got space, I got lifestyle – a La-Z-Boy chair, beer. I feel better. You could almost say they've made me comfortable. Almost too comfortable, you say?

FAT MAN gets up and locks his door with a few different kinds of locks.

That's why I lock the door. I don't know why I do it, but I do. It's psychological. It makes me feel safe. It gives me an edge I can set my beer on. Even though I know it's coming. I'm comfortable with it coming with the doors locked.

The TV suddenly turns on. The high-pitched sound of a TV test pattern. The multicoloured test pattern showing the head of an Indian chief appears on the screen. The high-pitched sound of the TV test pattern transforms into the seer-singing of THE DENE SEER.

FAT MAN stops and slowly looks over his shoulder at the image of the Indian chief on his TV.

FAT MAN
Oh … shit.

KOJI bends down to the trout on the ground below the cherry tree of hope.

LABINE BROTHER TWO
Listen, I'm getting out of here. These noises are getting too loud. It's trying to tell us something.

LABINE BROTHER ONE
You're trying to tell me you're scared of success. Scared of finally making good. What do you really know about that old scary Indian, anyways? In my experience, Indians are always telling stories. Trouble is they don't know when a story should end and reality should begin.

FAT MAN turns around and finally marches up to the TV and turns it off.

KOJI

I should never have dropped you, trout. It is a bad sign.

LABINE BROTHER TWO

Indians think different than we do.

LABINE BROTHER ONE

That's an understatement. You think I want to stay here in the dark? I'm here for mankind.

KOJI delicately touches the dying trout.

FAT MAN looks around the space and at the TV, daring it to come on.

The sound of a phonograph needle clunking down.

SONG

I was a fool to wander astray.
Straight is the gate and narrow is the way.
Now I have traded the wrong for the right.
Praise the Lord, I saw the light.

KOJI

I'll tell you a secret, trout. They say many people just before they die call out to their mothers even if those mothers have been dead for a long time, even if the one dying is very old.

LABINE BROTHER TWO

What you talking about?

LABINE BROTHER ONE
This black ore. This black ore that those Indians been
tiptoeing around from the beginning of everything.
What do you think this black rock might be?

LABINE BROTHER TWO
How do I know?

KOJI
The sound of light is coming; it's forming in my mouth.

LABINE BROTHER ONE
Radium. And you know what radium can do? It can cure
the world of cancer. We're out here 'cause we're gonna
discover the radium for radiation treatments.

KOJI
Pika.

LABINE BROTHER ONE
Yellow radium deep inside the black rock that can help
the world. You wanna help the world, or don't yah?

LABINE BROTHER TWO
Yeah. I guess, if you put it that way. What about the
Indian? I mean, shouldn't we give him a piece of the claim?

KOJI
I will call out for my grandmother because she loved me
and grew me to be a man.

*LABINE BROTHER ONE walks over to his brother
and places his arm around his shoulder.*

FAT MAN walks around the space looking for a logical explanation. He looks back at the dark face of the TV.

LABINE BROTHER ONE

What's an Indian gonna do with money? Don't you worry, he'll get his piece, all right … we'll give him some lard and baking powder and he can bake some bread. Sure! What the hell! What the hell is an Indian going to do with a rock anyways, at least he can eat the bread.

KOJI stands paralyzed with his eyes closed.

The song fades into a heartbeat under.

Lights up on a trail of white flour that forms a huge white circle. ROSE, finally still, stands in front of a small table and begins to set up her bread-making ingredients. She sloppily opens the flour sack. She takes a measuring cup and begins to count the cups of flour into a bowl.

FAT MAN begins to walk apprehensively toward the TV.

KOJI

Ichi.

ROSE

"Sit in the parlour" … my Irish father would say when the Indians came. The Indians, the relatives of my mother … Sitting aunties, uncles, and cousins quietly waiting in the parlour for their sister-cousin blood relative.

KOJI
Ni …

ROSE
Their red feet never touching the floorboards of our cabin. Never touching us, the half-breeds, breeded to be more European than someone from Europe. Bred to be white in the Indian-est of land.

KOJI
San.

ROSE
They would touch her then. Us, looking from the cracks of our skin, peeking through the door. Wanting to touch them like we seen the other Indian kids running straight into the stomachs of grown-ups, hugging and laughing.

KOJI
Obachan.

ROSE begins to cry.

ROSE
Damn it! … Excuse me.

The TV flashes on and shows the multicoloured test pattern with the head of an Indian chief. The high-pitched sound of THE DENE SEER seer-singing continues through the following scene.

FAT MAN stops in his tracks.

The sound of the LABINE BROTHERS' running footsteps. They take their flashlights and wave them around the dark space until the beams of light finally rest on their discovery.

LABINE BROTHER ONE

Come on … Goddamn it! I think I see something up there on the cliff. Oh Jesus … it's glowing …

They stand staring up paralyzed with their find.

Jesus … oh … Jesus … from the blackest black. Goddamn me sweet black. Black that can see like …

KOJI opens his eyes and looks up at his death discovery.

An atomic detonation lights up the space with a fierce light.

FAT MAN, shaken, runs toward the TV and shuts it off.

ROSE looks down and mixes the liquid with the dry ingredients.

ROSE

Two substances meeting like magic.

The glowing explodes.

The sound of wind.

The flour whirls everywhere.

KOJI

Pika Don.

The huge brightness evaporates to darkness except for one radiant light where LITTLE BOY sits huddled at the centre of the earth.

The sound of static during the broadcast of CBC Radio's National News Bulletin. The strange, thudding sound of a heart beating in the background.

RADIO ENGINEER (*voiceover*)
> Lorne, could you give us a level please.

LORNE GREENE/VOICE OF DOOM (*voiceover*)
> One … two … three … four … This will be the CBC, okay?

RADIO ENGINEER (*voiceover*)
> We need more copy, Mr. Greene.

LORNE GREENE/VOICE OF DOOM (*voiceover*)
> I am warming up to be the Voice of Doom. Here is a summary of the day's news. On this day, in our time, radium-rich ore was discovered on the Great Bear Lake in the Northwest Territories by two prospecting brothers, Gilbert and Charles LaBine.

LITTLE BOY
> Sometimes what you discover in the dark is not what you expected from the darkness. That the monster under the bed, or in the closet or coming up the stairs of your mind, is not the real monster. The real monster is the light of these discoveries.

LABINE BROTHER ONE reaches down and picks up the Indian boy-man. The sound of footsteps echoes as they walk out of the dark space, leaving complete and uncomfortable darkness.

The sound of the intro to "The Band Played On" from the 1940s. The sound of a sexy, older voice warming up.

ROUND ROSE (*voiceover*)

Hey, soldiers, how are my victims tonight? Here we are huddled together in the dark like two Orphan Annies. I'll show you mine if you show me yours. You can call me Tokyo Rose if I can call you bonehead. Does "I Saw the Light" stir up any memories, or haven't you boneheads any memories either? Now what memory holds your regret in the dark? Does it come when the lights are out and those you love have gone before you like a silent witness? Does it reach up when the dark gets loud and whisper the truth in your ear like a good mother after death? Can you feel me right here beside you? I can feel you inside me ... I mean, beside me. We are all lined up in the same orphanage of the world. Are you feeling pretty? Are you blond enough for someone to love you? Is your skin light enough for someone to save you? Questions in the dark never get answered, they just get wider as we get older. Here, now, don't be afraid. I'm here. Can you feel me? Can you feel me putting my hand on yours? In the dark, we are all from the same mother. Anywho ... sayonara.

RARE EARTH ELEMENTS

– Movement Two –

Characters begin to interact with the elements of their environment. Place and time. Caribou herds moving across the earth space. Depth and width between the surface.

The sound of hoof beats, small feet, fire, and whispers.

ROSE's white-flour circle becomes a huge circular compass shining up from the darkness. THE RADIUM PAINTER enters, the heels of her shoes clicking as she walks. She is a bright golden blonde dressed in a pale yellow dress from the 1930s. She takes her paintbrush from her painting kit and begins to paint the face of the compass in degrees, dipping the paintbrush in radium paint, and licking the tip of the brush with each stroke. She paints throughout.

From the centre of the circle, THE MINER clicks on the light of his miner's hat.

THE MINER

Shit … I'm way down. Not just this feeling of being beneath the earth but this feeling a guy gets when he's been there for awhile. I was thinking I might get married, not today or anything but after, when I get out of here and take a bath. Lots of women would think of marrying me, if they got to know me, because I got a job. Being down here is lonely; even if there's other guys down here it seems the space between us could tunnel to China. I think a lot about women down here. We only got four of them here in Port Radium. We call 'em Sandwich Queens 'cause they make our sandwiches and they make some guys' beds … if you know what I mean. I had my eyes on one of those Sandwich Queens. A good girl, she makes good sandwiches. I'm a good dancer. Gals like that. Anyways, this one has got real nice calves and makes a good ham sandwich. Next time I take a bath I just might ask her to dance so she can see my sensitive side. I'd say something like: "Excuse me, Missus, I've been noticin' you have some real healthy gams … could I have this dance?" Maybe I should forget the hams, gams … anyways …

He rolls up his work pants above his knees and acts like the woman.

And she might say, "Why, yes, that's mighty observant of you, Mr. … ?" (*answering as himself*) You can call me a miner. (*as woman*) "That's mighty sensitive of you, Mr. Miner, can I make your bed?" … I … uh … I … anyways, I got ahead of myself as usual.

He looks up as the sound of caribou hooves stampede across the surface of the earth. As he looks back down, THE WIDOW looks in her deep-red fire and then to the firelight shadows that dance up and take the shape of several men talking in a circle.

The sound of the radio dial gliding over static until it tunes in on a Dene announcer talking in Slavey on CBC Radio. The announcer is reading messages from people who are calling their loved ones home.

THE WIDOW bends her face into the fire, clutching a piece of clothing. She tries to let it go into the fire but brings it back to her chest. Across the space the white face of ROSE looks on.

SLAVEY ANNOUNCER (*voiceover*)
Hey, naga-tack-oh-tay, Art, why did you have to leave so soon? Your family loves you and wants you to know they are waiting in Fort Norman. There is a landscape of caribou coming …

One of the shadow-men waves his hand in recognition. The sound of his flickering response.

THE WIDOW
We used to be able to tell where we were by the seasons, the way the sun placed itself or didn't, the migration patterns of the caribou. Time.

She places the clothing over the fire and brings it back to her chest.

By the way we dressed, or how we dressed or undressed the ones we loved. Time.

She smells the clothing.

I remember the way he smelled. Women are always criticizing the smell of a man but I miss his smells, all of them. I miss the smell of sweat on his clothes after a long day hunting. I miss how the land stayed in the fabric even when he got inside the cabin. I miss helping him take his clothes off. Sounds funny now, at this age, talking about taking a man's clothes off but I miss the ritual of it. Taking off the layers to get to his skin. Taking his parka off. Taking his sweater off his arms as he raised them like a boy-child. Sitting down as he took his pants off and handed them to me. Both of us unwrapping his mukluks and pulling out each limb. I miss him sitting there with that grin I would trace with my fingers and then put my face on his chest, smell him so good because he was good, and he was mine. Smell his neck, eyes, and hands. Smell him so good I would cry sometimes because it was the smell of love. You never forget that smell. I wonder now if his spirit has skin. I want to smell him.

> *The thudding sound of a sack falling to the ground in FAT MAN's space.*

THE MINER
> Hello? Is anyone there? … okay.

> *From the dark, FAT MAN calls out.*

FAT MAN
> Who's there?

> *FAT MAN's TV turns on suddenly to reveal a Canadian loon in all its glory. The sound of loon calls.*

From the light of the broadcast, we see FAT MAN sitting in his chair, eating a big bowl of Kraft Dinner, and sipping his beer. In front of the TV is a sack.

FAT MAN

Shit, what's that? Now what? First an Indian and now a loon. Here, let me get up from my Kraft Dinner, from a long day … from my La-Z-Boy chair … all set up for the night … and see what the hell … is in front of my goddamn TV.

FAT MAN walks toward the sack and pushes it with his foot. LITTLE BOY appears.

I wasn't kidding … either an Indian or a loon. Okay, let me think … Indian. Loon. Indian. I don't get it.

The sound of static from the TV and the multicoloured test pattern with the head of an Indian chief appears. FAT MAN looks at the Indian chief and back at LITTLE BOY.

I get it … what I'm supposed to learn here is there is no such thing as one Indian.

LITTLE BOY

I want to go home.

FAT MAN

Not so fast … before we worry about your needs, how the hell did you get in here? I locked the door.

LITTLE BOY

I don't know locked doors.

FAT MAN

Very funny.

LITTLE BOY

I want to go home.

FAT MAN

Well, I'll let you in on a little-known secret. We all want
to go home. Even when we are home, we want to go
home. I guess we all got a place in our mind that isn't
exactly what we're living. This is not exactly what I had
imagined for myself but it buys the beers.

LITTLE BOY

I want to go home.

FAT MAN

Shit, are we in a bomb shelter here? Do you want me to
talk louder, play a little duck and cover … You're almost
naked. Do you know you're almost naked?

*He throws LITTLE BOY a T-shirt and a pair of big
pants from a laundry basket beside his La-Z-Boy.*

Here, put this on. I was hoping for maybe a little
company. Female company. But where a child is, a
woman is sure to follow. So young man. So what brings
you to my living room?

LITTLE BOY points to the TV.

Of course … the TV.

LITTLE BOY

Home. I want to go home.

FAT MAN

> Okay … we already did that.

LITTLE BOY

> I want to go back inside. I want to go home.

> *FAT MAN looks at the kid and hands him a bowl of
> Kraft Dinner.*

FAT MAN

> Who doesn't want to go back inside. Inside WHAT is the
> question? All I got is this hole. We are all in a hole if that
> makes you feel better. All of us. You, me, everyone. The
> hole is getting bigger. Now, I didn't say because us people
> were getting bigger, us people, Americans. I said, "The
> hole is getting bigger, deeper."

> *LITTLE BOY begins to play with the Kraft Dinner,
> taking the pieces and sticking them on the side of
> the chair.*

Like we are digging a hole so deep none of us will be able
to get in, or out, because the hole is getting filled with all
those immigrants: Asians and Pakistanis and Hindus and
Indians. I'm no racist; I'm just saying nobody knows
their place. Nobody knows they've been conquered. They
just keep it coming. Stretching the hole deeper with
immigration, and retribution. Soon there's nothing left.

> *LITTLE BOY nods.*

You hear that? Pretty soon … Nothing left. Shit, I should
write a song and get a bunch of hippies on a mountain
holding hands so they could sing … "We are the world,
we are the people" … We are the fuckin' hole. We have

made it big … and it's getting bigger, and bigger, talking to little Do Suzie Wong down the street, having to listen to Little Bear in the sticks, getting bigger, growing a big, empty auditorium where we can all sit down together and cry, fornicate our genes, and blow the fuckin' place out of the universe.

FAT MAN finally looks at LITTLE BOY, who has used the Kraft Dinner to write a big orange and glowing theoretical equation across the back of the chair: $e = mc^2$.

FAT MAN

What are you, a wise guy or something? Pick that shit up off the La-Z-Boy. For Chrissakes, what do you think this is? And put those clothes on … what are you, some kind of savage or something … By the way, he's not my kid, he belongs to the world. You know, he dances to a different drummer …

In the multicoloured test pattern, the Indian chief begins to talk in Slavey. THE DENE SEER Story One.

LITTLE BOY gets as close to the sound of the story as he can and begins to sound out the Slavey words.

Now that's what I call multimedia.

The sound of a typewriter. Stop. Roll. Crunch.

KOJI sits on his branch of the cherry tree. Across the space, ROUND ROSE sits at a small desk in front of a typewriter. She is in her mid-twenties, dressed very 1940s American Japanese. Her hair is in carefully braided pigtails. Scrunched pieces of paper at her feet.

She takes a white sheet of paper and rolls it into the typewriter. She begins to type.

KOJI

I am waiting here for my Obachan. Waiting like I used to wait when I was a child and the winds blew and the waters rose. Separated by elements, I would make my way here to this high ground. The highest ground. This cherry tree. When I got separated from my small world, I always knew to come to this place.

ROUND ROSE

Dear America, how are you? I am fine. I am waiting for you on Japanese soil. I know you will recognize me when you see me. We will look at each other – one American to another. Me a Californian bright. A UCLA graduate. You, my homeland. I am wearing my hair parted and braided just like I used to wear it when I was a university girl on campus. I am wearing this new suit here buttoned and lengthened just so, like an American suit dressed for a second chance. I look just like you, like me.

KOJI

Hold onto this one branch, you said. A higher branch of hope, you meant. Am I dead, Obachan? If I am dead, will you still come even though you know deep inside your bones you have carried me for the last time? Did you write me a note, Obachan, one last note /

ROUND ROSE

/ P.S. I am stoic. It is my nature to believe things will work out.

KOJI

In a landscape of notes.

ROUND ROSE

Sincerely yours, your true American daughter, Tokyo
Rose.

*ROUND ROSE takes the white paper from the
typewriter and signs her name. She waits politely with
the paper in hand.*

KOJI

There are notes left on anything that still exists. On
pieces of houses, on stones shivering on the ground, on
anything that did not perish, that will not perish. Hope.

ROUND ROSE

I will wait.

She begins to delicately fold the paper.

KOJI

Small notes appear across the landscape, nailed or
pinned onto surviving pieces of the blast. Hopeful
reminders to the lost ones who we are still waiting for.

ROUND ROSE

They will recognize me.

KOJI

That even in this hell someone will come back for us to
take us to safety; even in this charred landscape of hell,
hope remains nailed to what has survived.

ROUND ROSE

They will know who I am because I love them.

KOJI

Hope remains nailed to what has survived … a tin box of pictures, a rock wall, a rice bowl …

ROUND ROSE

I am not Japanese. No Japanese words ever suited my mouth properly. No Japanese taste ever tasted like my childhood.

KOJI

… a chair, a typewriter, a neighbour, a woman.

ROUND ROSE

I am American.

KOJI

I am nothing now and yet inside my self that no longer exists I am still Japanese. I am nothing and yet I know who I am.

ROUND ROSE bows her head.

The sound of fire.

The shadows of the fire reach high in the shape of men talking in a circle.

The sound of the radio dial gliding over static until it tunes in on a Dene announcer talking in Slavey on CBC Radio. The announcer reads messages from people who are calling their loved ones home.

ROSE stands covered in white flour, watching THE WIDOW.

SLAVEY ANNOUNCER (*voiceover*)

Hey, naga-tack-ohtay, Bertram, why don't you come home? Your family missing you now. I miss you. Come home now … We miss you like crazy …

One of the men turns up and bends his head. He responds through the fire: "I miss you too / soltenayay-ghay, ahquay, nagawhayta-ta-la, na-too,nagawhay,nagawhatt, mussi-nahwah."

THE WIDOW

Why you standing way over there? Why don't you come closer so I can get a good look at you.

ROSE begins to walk toward her with caution.

ROSE

How did you know I was here?

THE WIDOW

I can feel your eyes looking in.

ROSE

I'll just stand here if that's fine.

THE WIDOW

That's fine. Stuck up. Why you wanna come with your funny flour face looking? Don't even have the decency to wash your face before you see mine.

ROSE

I am baking bread.

THE WIDOW

How'd it get on your face?

ROSE

A gust of wind came through the door when I was
making bread. The flour flew up and I tried to catch it
with my sticky hands, and anyway I wiped my face and it
just stuck and made me laugh.

THE WIDOW

Well, you're not making me laugh. I thought you were
one of those white ghosts or, worse, a white woman
coming. What's your name anyways?

ROSE

Rose.

THE WIDOW looks at her.

I am Métis.

THE WIDOW

I know, you don't have to tell me. I can tell by the way the
white sticks to your bones.

ROSE

Oh …

THE WIDOW

Oh … don't get that look.

ROSE

What look?

THE WIDOW

Like I stepped on your sled-dog's tail.

ROSE

I just wanted to ask you if …

THE WIDOW
>If I knew your mother. Just because I'm an old widow
>doesn't mean I know everybody that's dead.

ROSE
>I thought maybe you might know her because she came
>from these parts.

THE WIDOW
>What, you think I know everybody's mother in
>the world?

ROSE
>No. Sorry. I just …

>>*ROSE begins to walk away.*

THE WIDOW
>So why you making bread, Miss Bread Maker?

ROSE
>I'm making bread for my father's store. We sell it to the
>men on the boats bringing up supplies on the Mackenzie.

THE WIDOW
>How much you sell it for?

ROSE
>A whole dollar.

THE WIDOW
>You gonna get rich like those LaBine Brothers wanna be.
>They should be prospecting bread instead of putting
>their hands on things that shouldn't be touched. Your
>father own the store?

ROSE

Yes, the H.B.C. store in Fort Norman.

THE WIDOW

You mean the Half Breed Curse store. Or the HERE BEFORE CHRIST store.

ROSE

I don't know.

THE WIDOW

Oh, don't get that look. You gotta have thicker skin. Look how thick my skin is. All right. The Hudson's Bay Store … seemed like they been here before Christ but not before me. Not before me.

ROSE

What are you doing sitting here by the fire?

THE WIDOW

I'm listening.

ROSE

I don't understand.

THE WIDOW

I think you do. Can you still hear your mother sing?

ROSE

Yes.

THE WIDOW

Good. She had a good voice.

*ROSE walks quietly away from the fire. She stands at
her bread table aggressively making dough.*
*THE MINER looks her way and shines his flashlight
on her white face and table.*

ROSE

If my mother was here I could've learned to sing, but
instead I am learning to make my father's bread. Flour,
yeast, salt, sugar, lard, liquid. Bread. It's not a pretty song.
Not like the colour yellow or the thought of my mother
singing, but it is all I will ever know. Flour, yeast, salt,
sugar, lard, liquid. Bread. She died when I was young,
before I had time to grab onto the hem of her dress and
hold on forever. She died because she was delicate, that
was all he ever said. The secret of good bread making is
to select your ingredients with care and to master a few
simple skills. Flour, yeast, salt, sugar, lard, liquid. Bread.
Don't let the long list of ingredients frighten you.

THE MINER

Hey, what's that?

ROSE

My mother went to Montreal to become a nun. She came
back a woman understanding a nun couldn't help the
Indians. Only a woman could.

Silence.

THE MINER

I said who's that?

*Silence, and then she slams the dough down and
kneads it.*

ROSE (*she laughs*)

Flour, yeast, salt, sugar, lard, liquid. Bread.

THE MINER

Come on, you're starting to give me the heebie-jeebies.

ROSE

Don't let the long list of ingredients frighten you.

THE MINER

What is that?

ROSE

Mixing, kneading, rising, punching down, shaping loaves. She saved my father, the Irishman, softening him from a journey of Irish potatoes, Indian curries, and Chinese noodles. He was a stowaway at fourteen on a clipper that travelled the Orient and by accident discovered my Indian mother. Letting loaves rise. By accident, she discovered me. Letting loaves cool.

THE MINER

Excuse me?

She touches herself like a loaf of bread.

ROSE

This perfect loaf of bread is plump with a rounded body and straight sides. I have a tender, golden-brown crust that can be crisp, or delicate. This grain is fine and even, with slightly elongated cells; the flesh of this bread is multi-grained. You never know what you're going to look like. Some say it's in the current. Others say, if you're mixed and from Canada, it's in the currency of blood.

She wipes her white face and hands until they are brown skin.

THE MINER

I said is anybody out there?

ROSE

Flour, yeast, sugar, salt, lard, liquid. Bread. Don't let the long list of ingredients frighten you.

She moulds a perfect loaf of dough and throws it up into the darkness.

The sound of ROUND ROSE's chair scraping back as she stands up. Her letter is folded in a neat square and pinned to her lapel. She begins to exit. She stops, reaches down, and grabs a small square note left on the ground. She unfolds it and reads it softly in English at the same time that THE JAPANESE GRANDMOTHER reads it in Japanese.

THE JAPANESE GRANDMOTHER (*voiceover*)

Koji, Obachan da yo. Kono sakura no ki ni renraku-dayori o oitoku kara, ne. Wakaretara so surutte iutta desho.

ROUND ROSE

Koji, it is your grandmother. I have left this note here on the cherry tree like I used to do when we were separated. I have left this note to let you know I am still looking for you. I am old and need to believe I will see your face. I waited here for as long as I could. The fire is coming now. Safe journey to you, my grandson.

ROUND ROSE pins it back on the tree and exits.

From the dark sky, a loaf of bread falls.

KOJI

Safe journey to you, Obachan.

Koji looks up as the loaf of bread falls through the darkness ...

Ikoyo!

KOJI lets go of his cherry tree and dives to catch the loaf, disappearing from his world into the darkness in-between as he begins his journey.

The sound of caribou herds travelling over space.

THE MINER listens as the sound of the hooves of the caribou herd pass and then as THE RADIUM PAINTER clicks through the mine.

THE MINER

I can hear you so you might as well talk.

THE RADIUM PAINTER

I'm sorry, I didn't mean to scare you; I just wanted to see ...

She walks into his miner's light.

THE MINER

See ... See what?

THE RADIUM PAINTER

I just wanted to see the mine.

THE MINER

Oh ... Why?

THE RADIUM PAINTER

I'm just curious is all.

THE MINER

Women aren't supposed to be down here, you know? It can be dangerous. But I guess they can be curious.

THE RADIUM PAINTER

I'm here now so … I need to know where it comes from. The radium. I want to know.

THE MINER

Well, okay … I guess if you're here already there's no harm. But this is secret. Our secret, okay?

She nods as she draws closer to him.

When you're mining the vein, it creates a pit. Some of these pits have shafts to the surface. Like this place here in Port Radium. Shafts up to the surface after diamond drilling. It's called pitchblende.

THE RADIUM PAINTER

Pitchblende.

THE MINER

Well, that's when it's raw, are you listening to me? You got kinda a funny look on your face.

THE RADIUM PAINTER

I thought it was called radium?

THE MINER

You're right, but right in the mine surface when you're mining it, it comes out pitchblende. Then it has to be refined into uranium and radium. Arsenic separates it.

She looks up at the darkness and then moves slightly toward him. Nervously, he talks.

It's black – jet black – black like coal. Shiny black coal.
Who did you say you were?

THE RADIUM PAINTER
I didn't.

THE MINER
You don't look anything like those Sandwich Queens up
top. You look ...

THE RADIUM PAINTER
Yes? Do you think I look pretty?

THE MINER
You look like you got a good set of hams. I mean gams.
Oh ... sh ... You got nice legs and ... anyways ... Want to
hear a funny thing? A driller was telling me one time,
that I shouldn't be playing around with too much of that
black ore, especially in the bottom area, because I could
go sterile.

   She just looks at him.

I mean, not that I'm suggesting anything crazy here. I
just was making, trying ... to fill in the conversation. The
driller was probably just saying that to scare me. We wear
rubber pants anyway.

THE RADIUM PAINTER
Rubber pants ... Like a baby.

THE MINER
No, geez. What'd I say? Let's talk about something else.
Like, geez, you sure are pretty. It's like you glow, you are
so beautiful.

She starts to back away and runs.

I mean I didn't mean anything by it. We can talk about the mine. It's a wet mine. Did I tell you that? Right under the Great Bear Lake. Hey, where you going? I should at least take you up. You shouldn't be running around here in the dark? Hey!

Silence.

THE MINER
Goddamnit! God damn my mouth, "especially in the bottom area because I could go sterile." Dumb. That girl shouldn't be down here anyways, what was I thinkin', talkin' about the mine to her, a guy could get arrested for talking about what's underground. A guy could get arrested for looking at her. A guy should take a cold shower. A guy should just shut up.

FAT MAN leans over and covers LITTLE BOY as he sleeps on the couch. He sits back down on his La-Z-Boy chair. FAT MAN looks at his living room.

The sound of the radio dial gliding over static until it tunes into the CBC Radio's National News Bulletin. The station fades in with the strange thudding sound of a heart beating in the background.

RADIO ENGINEER (*voiceover*)
Lorne, could you give us a level please.

LORNE GREENE/VOICE OF DOOM (*voiceover*)
One … two … three … four … This is the CBC, okay?

The frequency sound of another party line bleeding in. Small lights on ROUND ROSE as she sits on a piece of luggage, her hands bound, her body jailed, her voice still broadcasting.

ROUND ROSE

This is your old faithful friend, Tokyo Rose. Coming to you in your need even if you didn't come to me in mine.

The radio dial tunes back in.

RADIO ENGINEER (*voiceover*)

We need more copy, Mr. Greene.

LORNE GREEN/VOICE OF DOOM (*voiceover*)

This is the *National News Bulletin*. A summary of the day's news.

The frequency sound of another party bleeding in.

ROUND ROSE

Hey, boneheads …

The radio dial tunes back in.

RADIO ENGINEER (*voiceover*)

Lorne?

LORNE GREEN/VOICE OF DOOM (*voiceover*)

A group of scientists in Europe can now show that, when a uranium atom fissions, two or three extra neutrons are also given to go off. This important observation suggests that a self-sustaining chain reaction might …

ROUND ROSE

Yes? Get on …

The new copy begins to fade.

LORNE GREENE/VOICE OF DOOM (*voiceover*)
… that a self-sustaining chain reaction might get off …

ROUND ROSE
Thinking about me.

FAT MAN
A guy could get horny sitting all day, or should I say a guy could get uncomfortable. War is uncomfortable even if it is man-made. Sometimes I think I should get a wife. A perfect mate. A Frigidaire. A Lucy–Ricky thing that makes a little Ricky, but mostly I think I should get laid while thinking of death. It would be a heightened sexual experience, though, ultimately making me a more sensitive, understanding human being, who could then buy more appliances and other things I don't really need. I could get fucked while thinking of the evildoers and then go spend more money. Now that makes me hard.

FAT MAN touches himself at the thought.

*ROUND ROSE stands up and, as she does,
she projects herself as TOKYO ROSE –
the geisha girl–dragon woman in his mind.*

ROUND ROSE
Hey, soldier …

FAT MAN
I didn't touch it.

ROUND ROSE
Having a little party by yourself?

FAT MAN talks to ROUND ROSE but only sees the TOKYO ROSE shadow.

LORNE GREEN/VOICE OF DOOM (*voiceover*)
Ladies and gentlemen, this just in (and for a change most of the news is good). The U.S. government has ordered eight tons of uranium for military research from the Canadian company that owns and operates the Great Bear Mine.

ROUND ROSE
Bad soldier.

FAT MAN
Hey, I never touched it. I was just thinking about the end of the world and how it ... ah ... shit, how it makes me horny. I mean, how it makes me lonely.

ROUND ROSE
How lonely are you?

LORNE GREEN/VOICE OF DOOM (*voiceover*)
This is the *National News Bulletin*. The U.S government has ordered sixty tons of uranium with special permission from the Canadian government.

FAT MAN
I'm feeling so lonely I can feel the end of the world.

He lays his hand on his penis. He touches himself.

RADIO ENGINEER (*voiceover*)
We need more copy, Mr. Greene.

ROUND ROSE moans sexually under the following scene.

55

LORNE GREENE/VOICE OF DOOM (*voiceover*)
> This is the *National News Bulletin*. A summary of today's news. U.S. and Canadian governments join forces in the effort to get uranium from Eldorado Mines in Port Radium to Eldorado's Refinery in Port Hope, Ontario, to the United States' Manhattan Project. The U.S. Army has ordered another 350 tons of uranium.

ROUND ROSE
> Now that's big.

> *The copy begins to fade.*

LORNE GREENE/VOICE OF DOOM (*voiceover*)
> This just in (but not really because it is a war secret).

ROUND ROSE
> Secrets. Are you making yourself homesick, soldier? Thinking about your wife back home going out with your friends – both of them?

FAT MAN
> That's great. Great.

ROUND ROSE
> Thinking about them doing it in your kitchen as they look at their proud bodies reflected in the chrome toaster and kettle …

FAT MAN
> Yes … yes …

ROUND ROSE
> Pumping the chrome kitchen table till it rocks off its shiny feet. How's that?

FAT MAN

Talk about the chrome. The chrome. Oh God, the chrome …

ROUND ROSE

Somebody's got to clean that you know.

FAT MAN

Yeah … yeah … the chrome … the chrome …

The sound of the mike clicking off. The shadow of TOKYO ROSE diminishes. ROUND ROSE turns and carries her suitcase on her journey.

LITTLE BOY

I want to go home.

FAT MAN

I'm just about turning into the driveway … if I could get a little … quiet here.

LITTLE BOY

Now.

He reaches into his pocket and grabs a handful of cash and throws it at LITTLE BOY.

FAT MAN

Christ, here, take a Greyhound … what do I care. Buy a yo-yo … go somewhere.

LITTLE BOY takes the money and places it on the coffee table. The test pattern with the Indian chief comes on. LITTLE BOY sits cross-legged close to it, looking in.

FAT MAN

You're gonna go blind sitting so close to the TV. Fuck, what do I care ... just don't look over here. I'm doing something important.

He places his hand back on his crotch.

Chrome ... chrome, we were talking about chrome. I'm homesick, remember. Ahhh ... shit ... so close and yet so far.

FAT MAN falls asleep snoring post-almost sex.

In the multicoloured test pattern, the Indian chief begins to talk in Slavey as LITTLE BOY hums underneath, listening to THE DENE SEER Story Two.

THE WIDOW's fire gets brighter, lighting her as she sleeps, cuddling a shirt and pants. The two rubber boots stand by.

The group of tall fire shadows whispers softly, encouragingly: "Go on now." ... Finally a real man's body appears, covered in flames. He talks to his wife, THE WIDOW, as she sleeps.

DENE ORE CARRIER

Psss ... My girl, pass me my pants ... I have to go to work. I can't go to work with no pants, now can I? My girl ... are you dreaming of me, 'cause I'm dreaming of you.

THE WIDOW begins to stir in her sleep.

THE WIDOW

Go back to sleep. It is too early for you to get up. It is too early for you to leave.

DENE ORE CARRIER

I got a job and I can't go naked.

THE WIDOW

Why?

DENE ORE CARRIER

Do you want everyone to laugh? Look at that Sahtu Dene with no pants on. Is that how they work those natives here? Besides, I am working for the white man. It is best to wear all the clothes I can. Besides, even the caribou would laugh.

THE WIDOW gets up and sleep-talks.

THE WIDOW

You got to put your boots on first.

DENE ORE CARRIER

Why?

THE WIDOW

Because you do if you ever want to see your pants.

He puts his rubber boots on and stands in the fire.

DENE ORE CARRIER

There. Here I am. A Sahtu Dene in nothing but rubber boots.

THE WIDOW begins to laugh as a young woman.

THE WIDOW

You look good. A white man's company should be proud to have you.

DENE ORE CARRIER

Give me my pants.

THE WIDOW

No.

DENE ORE CARRIER

Give me my shirt then. I have to go to work. My girl, I have to go to work. It is the only job in these parts. Do you want to starve?

THE WIDOW

There are plenty of trout and caribou to last us till we die.

DENE ORE CARRIER

Times are changing, my girl. Times are changing and we have to change with them or be left behind. It is for our family.

THE WIDOW

Here, take your shirt then, it's against my better mind. But if you're gonna be so charming, what chance do I have.

She gets up and puts his shirt on.

He takes her scarf off her head and touches her hair.

DENE ORE CARRIER

You are as beautiful as the day I married you.

She smells him.

THE WIDOW

You are ... you smell so, so ...

He picks her up and throws her over his shoulder and twirls her around in the shadows of the firelight.

DENE ORE CARRIER

You are my woman and I will carry those sacks of ore like a strong Dene man can.

He sets her down.

THE WIDOW

Okay, you can have the pants. But never your caribou-hide jacket.

He grabs and begins to turn.

Aren't you gonna put your pants on?

DENE ORE CARRIER

Let them talk, my girl ...

She laughs.

He disappears laughing into the fire shadows of men.

THE WIDOW stands as she wakes, calling into the fire. The rubber boots, shirt, and pants are in the fire about to perish.

THE WIDOW

Did I tell you I love you, my man? Did I tell you I love you every day?

The sound of caribou herds moving.

The sound of THE RADIUM PAINTER's frantic, clicking footsteps.

THE MINER looks up and then …

THE MINER
What are you doing here again? I thought you left.

THE RADIUM PAINTER
You took a bath.

THE MINER
A shower, compliments of the Great Bear Lake leaking.
You shouldn't be here.

THE RADIUM PAINTER
There's nowhere I can go.

> *The sound of a needle hitting a record. The sound of
> "Indian Love Song" from the 1940s filters in.*

Could you hold me? Just for a minute or two? I'm scared.

THE MINER
Come here, darling, there's nothing to be frightened of.

They begin to dance slowly to the music.

THE RADIUM PAINTER
I just wanted to know if I could give it back. If I could
leave it here underground so no one would have to know
what I know. See what I know inside.

THE MINER
Leave what here, darling?

THE RADIUM PAINTER
This paint.

He reaches down and helps her let the paintbox fall to the ground. His hand takes the earth and buries the paintbox. He stands and reaches under her chin and kisses her beautifully.

THE MINER
Everything's buried here. Every secret that begins here, ends here. You hear me? Everything's going to be all right.

LITTLE BOY gets closer to the multicoloured test pattern with the Indian chief. LITTLE BOY rests his forehead on the image.

He backs up from the TV and the multicoloured Indian chief has become more human, less TV-like. He is THE DENE SEER.

LITTLE BOY smiles.

LITTLE BOY
Neg-o-tach-otay? How do you feel?

The sound of caribou herds running.

WATERWAYS

– Movement Three –

The movement of scenes through, under, and over dangerous waters. Worlds swirling in brief currents that throw them together and then separate.

The sound of Dene and Japanese drums submerging in and out of the static of propaganda, the sound score of Western civilization building a country.

THE DENE SEER (*voiceover*)

Can you read the air? The face of the water? Can you look through time and see the future? Can you hear through the walls of the world? Maybe we are all talking at the same time because we are answering each other over time and space. Like a wave that washes over everything and doesn't care how long it takes to get there because it always ends up on the same shore.

The talking of THE DENE SEER floats through and fades.

Way above, inside the small window of the pilothouse on the Radium Prince, a big Icelandic man stands before his steering wheel, swinging it right and left of the banks, sandbars, dangerous currents, and scenes below. He hollers instructions to the two men below.

THE TWO STEVEDORES stand below him, holding long poles that dip into the water's dark blueness and into the surface of scenes, raising the poles and lowering them into the changing depths of water as they make their way through the waterways, collecting sacks of uranium and placing them around the compass in degrees.

A dramatic gung-ho sound accompanies the river scenes as in a 1940s or '50s documentary.

CAPTAIN MIKE (*voiceover*)
Jesus Clist, I can read da face of des water and I tol' you guys to put da goddamn poles in da water if we wada to go anywhere dis goddamn century. I'm sittin' in da pilothouse of dis goddamn *Radium Prince* and, if we don't go nowhere in a goddamn hurry, we won't be goin' anywhere goddamn soon.

THE TWO STEVEDORES laugh and dip the poles into the water, into the dark surface.

THE TWO STEVEDORES
"If we don't go nowhere in a goddamn hurry, we won't be goin' anywhere goddamn soon."

They laugh.

CAPTAIN MIKE (*voiceover*)
You tink dis is funny? I'd like to see how funny you tink it is if we sink dis goddamn boat and everyting and every goddamn man, sack of goddamn uranium, and supplies goes down and you goddamn fellows just laughing like dis is some kind of goddamn picnic. Jesus Clist, if I have to hall my big Icelandic ass down der and do it myself, you better hope you can swim bedder than dose goddamn big trout you got in dis goddamn lake.

ONE STEVEDORE
Hol-ee! All he had to say was he was ready.

THE OTHER STEVEDORE
I was born ready.

ONE STEVEDORE
No you weren't, you were born in Fort Smith.

THE OTHER STEVEDORE
Never mind you.

ONE STEVEDORE
We're more than ready. Let's go!

CAPTAIN MIKE (*voiceover*)
Okay now, dat's bedder. Let's shove off. We only got forty-eight more miles to go, des goddamn sacks cruised to us from da Bear River Landing after dey rided de goddamn Great Bear Lake. It's our responsibility to taken dem down the Bear River, and dose poor assholes gotta handle dose sacks of ore, eighteen more times, nine miles around da Bear River Rapids, load dem goddamn sacks in a truck, and den one more goddamn barge, and takem tirty miles to Fort Norman, where we transfer dem to

anodder goddamn barge up da Mackenzie, across dat goddamn Great Slave Lake, and up da Slave River to Fort Smith, and den portages it again onto trucks and back into da boats up da Athabasca River to da goddamn Waterways, where it's put on a goddamn train, where we don't have to see des particular goddamn sacks, for da rest of our goddamn long days. You probably thinkin', Jesus Clist, it'd be easier da go to war and fight dose goddamn Germans. And today I think yor'd goddamn right. Let's get dis boat goin'.

> THE TWO STEVEDORES *plunge the poles in. They yell up. He yells back and the wheel turns rapidly.*
>
> THE TWO STEVEDORES *continue to carry the uranium sacks on the boat and place them in degrees.*
>
> ROSE *walks through with a paper-wrapped loaf of bread, heading toward* THE WIDOW, *who stares into the flames of the* DENE ORE CARRIERS, *listening to them talking and whispering back.*
>
> *The sound of the radio dial gliding over static until it tunes in on a Dene announcer talking in Slavey on CBC Radio. The announcer reads messages from people who are calling their loved ones home.*

SLAVEY ANNOUNCER (*voiceover*)
Hey, naga-tack-otay, Paul. We think of you everyday and thank you for being such a good father and husband. Bless you forever. Your daughter.

One of the fire shadows of the DENE ORE
CARRIERS reaches up and creates a man shadow
that flickers and whispers, "I love you / solten-
nayquaw-naganewwetoo,a-etaw-essey-etaw-essey-mu
ssi … nagawheyta."

ROSE

Hey …

ROSE comes to THE WIDOW and hands her the loaf.

THE WIDOW

What's this, a big rock?

ROSE

No, it's a loaf of bread I made.

THE WIDOW

It's heavy like the sacks of ore. Eighty pounds heavy it
feels like … No, geez almost one hundred and twenty
pounds this sack. Just like the ore carriers used to carry.
If I keep this up, I'm going to be an old bent-up woman
and fall in this fire. Is that what you want?

ROSE

Geez. I was just tryin to be neighbourly and give you a
loaf from my fresh batch.

THE WIDOW

So, Miss Stuck-Up Bread Maker, why'd I want to eat this?

ROSE

'Cause it's the best bread in these parts and … 'cause I
made it for you.

THE WIDOW

Let's take a good look at this uppity bread.

THE WIDOW uncovers it and smells it. ROSE begins to walk away.

Now where you goin'?

ROSE

I'm gettin' ready to go work on the boats. Cookin' for the men.

THE WIDOW

What's your father say about that … not having his number one bread maker to man the post?

ROSE

It was his idea. He thinks I might meet a good man. They're sending all sorts of men up North to help get the sacks of ore transported down. I guess he thinks I might meet myself a good man coming up.

THE WIDOW

What's wrong with our good men? I guess they call our good men "coolies." Okay … okay. I know. You better git cookin' before I go on. Bon voyage, or whatever.

ROSE (*in Slavey*)

Till then.

ROSE bends down and kisses THE WIDOW.
ROSE leaves.

THE WIDOW

Coolies. Some word for people that do the dirty work, I guess. The people that get their hands dirty. The coolies, the Indians, the Dene, the People – our men, my man, worked hauling those sacks, in long lines, from one man to the next, one coolie to one coolie, one Indian to another. A chain passing the rock. A rock we called the money rock.

A dramatic gung-ho sound accompanies the river scene.

Lights up on CAPTAIN MIKE and THE TWO STEVEDORES below. THE CAPTAIN begins to bellow from the pilothouse.

CAPTAIN MIKE (*voiceover*)
Jesus Clist, I tol' you guys to put da goddamn poles in da water if we wada to go anywhere dis goddamn century. Why'd I have to work in da only goddamn part of da country where da daylight hours in da day is da hol' goddamn day and nit. Twenty-four goddamn hours a day we gotta keep dis boat goin' and dose poor assholes gotta haul dose sacks. I'm sittin' in da pilothouse of dis goddamn *Radium Prince* and if we don't go nowhere in a goddamn hurry, we won't be goin' anywhere goddamn soon.

THE TWO STEVEDORES laugh and dip the poles into the water, into the dark surface.

THE TWO STEVEDORES (*mimicking*)
"If we don't go nowhere in a goddamn hurry, we won't be goin' anywhere goddamn soon."

CAPTAIN MIKE (*voiceover*)

You tink dis is funny? I'm tryin' to make a goddamn map
we can all navigate, but dis face of des wader changes
faster den a whore on payday ...

> *ROSE enters the space of the boat and folds out a
> table. She unpacks her ingredients and begins to set
> up her bread-making ritual. She looks up.*

Anyways, dis girl here is gonna cook us some food. All
you young fellows watch your goddamn ... your mouths
around da lady.

> *THE TWO STEVEDORES lower their poles and yell
> up. THE CAPTAIN spins the wheel. Slaps his arms
> and body.*

CAPTAIN MIKE (*voiceover*)

You probably thinkin', Jesus Clist, it'd be easier da go to
war den deal with des goddamn governments, and des
goddamn mosquitoes. You fellows don't have to go to
war because yor Indians and I'm on some special
goddamn war production act. And today, I'd like to tell
des goddamn mosquitoes to go fight dat goddamn Hitler,
and des goddamn governments to leave us bodth da
goddamn alone. Jesus Clist, I'm gonna bleed to death
from des blood sucking goddamn mosquitoes!

ONE STEVEDORE

What mosquitoes?

THE OTHER STEVEDORE

I don't feel no mosquitoes.

THE TWO STEVEDORES stand unbothered. They lower their poles and yell up.

CAPTAIN MIKE (*voiceover*)
Goddamnit, you fellows! Always messin' aroun'. Let's git this boat goin' before I have to come down der and …

CAPTAIN MIKE yells and swings the wheel and they vanish into the water.

The sound of the hyper-documentary drifts into different sounds as LITTLE BOY changes the TV channel and switches through the sounds and flickering light of TV shows from the 1950s. In the darkened living room, flashes of sound from Dragnet, Gunsmoke, Animal Kingdom, *and so on. Through the flickering light, FAT MAN lies sleeping in his La-Z-Boy chair.*

The sound of bugs getting it on on the nature channel.

FAT MAN starts to moan and then licks his lips in thirst as he wakes.

FAT MAN
Get me a beer, will ya? You think God, or Coca-Cola, would make a six-pack. Six is a good number to wake up to.

LITTLE BOY gets him a beer.

Ah … shit … Look at these goddamn cockroaches. You can't beat a bug or an Indian. I mean, they breed like rabbits, and if a big bomb were to come down on us right now, they'd be the only thing left. Pretty interesting, huh? Nothing to say, huh? What do you think about them

having sex right here in the living room on national
television.

LITTLE BOY
They look pretty.

FAT MAN
Like hell, they look like bugs fucking. The only thing
worse than a bug getting it, is me almost getting it and
then not getting it. Speaking of getting it. How many
rabbits you think are hidden on this can of beer? Come
on now, you look pretty Indian … How many rabbits on
this Old Style beer? These are men questions. Come on …

*LITTLE BOY gets closer and begins to count the
rabbits on the can. He finds eight.*

LITTLE BOY
Eight. Eight rabbits.

FAT MAN
Ten. Ten rabbits on the beer. See, look … One, two, three,
four, five, six, seven, eight, nine, ten. That's why I'm the
man and you're the boy. Don't worry, not many people
can find all of them. Here, have a sip … it will make you
feel better.

LITTLE BOY takes a sip.

Okay see here, these bugs just had sex, and now they're
eaten by another bigger bug. That's life. Survival of the
fittest … natural selection …

LITTLE BOY
Darwin.

FAT MAN

Exactly. If you can imagine the end of the world, you can imagine making the world end for someone else first. That's the theory. Christ, I'm no nuclear physicist – or anything. I'm just saying that way you can have a beer before it happens to you. You can turn on the TV, have a baby, teach them nothing, get a divorce, pay some alimony, get two jobs, work longer hours, have a beer, and hope for a heart attack so you won't have to give another cent to your ex-wife. The thing is, you can have another beer ... that's all I'm saying. I'm saying sooner or later, we're all going to die. The end of the world, the end of your world. On a hot day – it's the last beer that's gonna make it worth it. It's universal.

FAT MAN gets closer to LITTLE BOY and drunkenly tries to pull him in.

The sound of a needle being set down on a record.
The sound of the intro to "The Band Played On."

FAT MAN

Come here, kid. Come here, it's okay. I'm sorry. I'm getting drunk ... because I can. I mean, what good is it to be a dummy in a goddamn house that is a target, and you're supposed to sit here and look like a happy son of a bitch, knowing all along you're gonna be the first to get it. You see anybody from the government sitting here? No, they're the ones pushing the buttons and we're the ones sitting in our living rooms watching the goddamn news. Well fuck it, I'm ready. Bomb the goddamn place to shit. What do I care? I've come to some conclusions as a piece of shit. Fuck it. That's my conclusion. I'm gonna dream a little dream. I'm gonna get married. I'm gonna adopt you for Chrissakes. What do I care if you're an Indian and I'm, I'm, I'm, okay fuck, a white man, I guess. I'm gonna get married. I'm gonna get married to anyone who will marry me. Fuck it, we'll get a mommy, don't you worry. Don't you worry. I'll do all the worrying. Who in their right mind would marry me anyway? I'm a future has-been. Here, eat your processed cheese. What does a kid know?

FAT MAN takes a big swig of his beer. The huge shadow of TOKYO ROSE looms large on the walls.

ROUND ROSE (*voiceover*)
Greetings, soldiers. Did you miss me? Do you know what I know? Do you want to know what I know? If I tell you mine, will you tell me yours? Secrets between a man and a woman are like secrets between governments and money. Secrets between the sheets. So simple, these simple secrets that they sit in small, simple bedrooms and think they are important like a large dick in the desert. Am I telling you something you don't know? Look close … Look at me. What do you imagine when you imagine me? Could you imagine I was a woman who loved you? Could you imagine I wanted a family? A home? A husband? A baby? Could you imagine I was just a woman, not the enemy … just a woman?

A long pause. The sound of ROUND ROSE beginning to cry. FAT MAN looks directly at her for the first time and the TOKYO ROSE shadow disappears.

FAT MAN
Oh God, don't cry. Look here, me and the boy … we're here. We'll be your family. I've always loved you.

76

A long pause. ROUND ROSE turns and begins to walk toward them. FAT MAN grabs LITTLE BOY's hand as ROUND ROSE joins them to make a family.

You're home. You're finally home.

The sound of the radio dial gliding over static until it tunes in on a Dene announcer talking in Slavey on CBC Radio. The announcer reads messages from people who are calling their loved ones home.

SLAVEY ANNOUNCER (*voiceover*)
Hey, naga, tack-ohtay. We have brought the dogs in for the feast. Your grandchildren are getting real good at looking after them. I am so proud of them. You would be too. Love, your friend Ethel.

A flicker of a flame responds back, "I am proud of them too / ah,ah,sir-sa-la,goona-loon,a-la-lineta,sa-la-mussi."

THE WIDOW touches her husband's remaining things as the echoing sound of a tunnel begins to build under and KOJI begins to circle faster and faster between worlds.

THE WIDOW
This love of mine remembers the first day I met him like it was yesterday, but not quite yesterday, like it was almost a different life this yesterday. A vision so beautiful, so filled with love and complete that I can hardly recognize myself sitting here, or there. I am in parts, this life now hollow so his spirit can pass in front of me, whispering and drifting like smoke and staying like a shadow. It is always the little things of his that take

my breath away. The real things like one of his hairs lying on the collar of a caribou-hide jacket he loved … the real things like the handle of his hunting knife worn down from his beautiful hands that loved me. The real things … because then I know he was real, not a dream, and I know there is a tunnel between us. These real things can leave me down for so long that for days I can barely look up from the fire and into the sky's eyes. I don't know … love is long and hollow inside us, and some days, long days, it takes awhile to catch your breath.

She begins to cry.

The sound of a huge splash into water as KOJI finally lands in his new world.

The hyper-documentary sound of the river.

CAPTAIN MIKE (*voiceover*)
Jesus Clist, we've hit a goddamn fish. No, it's a goddamn asshole.

THE CAPTAIN is hauling the wheel back and forth trying to steady it.

THE TWO STEVEDORES try and haul KOJI up on a shaky boat.

Goddamn, get that trout pulled up now!

ONE STEVEDORE
It's heavy.

THE OTHER STEVEDORE
All the trouts are heavy here.

ONE STEVEDORE
Most are like a hundred pounds or so.

> *They go on talking and hauling him up as if he is a trout.*

THE OTHER STEVEDORE
As big as a man.

ONE STEVEDORE
But not as big as me.

THE OTHER STEVEDORE
Smarter though.

ONE STEVEDORE
You saying a trout is smarter than me?

THE OTHER STEVEDORE
I'm saying this trout is, because it's a man, stupid.

KOJI
Thank you.

ONE STEVEDORE
Mouthy too.

THE OTHER STEVEDORE
Where'd you fall from? We didn't see you go in.

KOJI
There was this light in the sky when I was talking to this trout and then I was flying and I landed on a branch and then I tried to grab a loaf of bread then and I was swimming and …

ONE STEVEDORE
    Must have hit his head good.

KOJI
    I fell from a branch.

ONE STEVEDORE
    My bet's he fell from the sky would be a better chance.

KOJI
    Well, the sky was falling too.

THE OTHER STEVEDORE
    You see the trees around here? You couldn't get up on a
    tree, never mind hold onto a branch here, Henny Penny.

KOJI
    Well, all I know is I let go.

ONE STEVEDORE
    Good enough for me.

KOJI
    It is?

ONE STEVEDORE
    Sure, what the hell.

THE OTHER STEVEDORE
    Stranger things have happened here.

CAPTAIN MIKE (*voiceover*)
    Jesus Clist, you tink we were havin' a polite tea pardy at
    da convent in Fort Franklin, and not on dis *Radium
    Prince*. If you ladies don't mind, we gotta go aways before
    you fellows can go on a goddamn date. You tink you can
    keep it in you goddamn pants till den?

THE TWO STEVEDORES howl. He points to KOJI,
the trout-boy.

Go downstairs and git da girl to find you some clothes …
and git you sometin' to eat … and watch your goddamn
mouth. She's a lady.

ROUND ROSE delicately opens her suitcase and
places her painted, white-faced Japanese dolls
throughout her new home.

Lights up on ROSE as she sits on the sacks of uranium
as if they are a stool. She gets up and stands at her
bread table. She begins to put her hands in the flour
and dough.

ROSE

Sometimes when I knead this bread I dream. Women are
always dreaming when their hands are busy. I dream I
could be anybody if I was born somewhere else.
Sometimes it makes you think what you could form out
of your own hands if people were big enough to accept
you for what you are – the depth of your dreams. I'm
grateful for having a job and everything, but sometimes I
want something more for myself, somewhere else.

ROSE moulds the dough into a flat mask and places it
on her face until she can no longer breathe under the
white mask.

Dumb.

She cries and then laughs at herself. She looks up at
KOJI, who is looking at her.

Where'd you come from?

KOJI

I was fishing.

ROSE

You a good fisherman?

KOJI

I used to think so.

ROSE

Then how come your clothes are wet?

KOJI

It's a long story. Where are we?

ROSE

We're just about to dock in Norman Wells. You want
some dry clothes or want to just stand there almost
naked?

KOJI

I'm sorry.

ROSE

It's all right. You know they say, these sacks of ore are
gonna cure cancer. Nobody knows what cancer is here,
but I guess you're talking about a people that don't even
know what war is. Do you know what cancer is?

KOJI

No.

ROSE

Well, they say that's why they started taking it out of the
mine anyways ... to cure cancer ... oh, and so that men

at war can see the face of their watches when it's dark.
But now they're in a big rush to make something big.

KOJI

The war's still on. You know about the war?

ROSE

Sure. I listen to the radio you know.

KOJI

Do you know where it is?

ROSE

No ... I don't care much either. It's none of my business.
It's men's business, some say white man's business.

KOJI

Oh.

ROSE

I'm making bread. Are you hungry?

KOJI

Yes.

ROSE

Are you cold?

KOJI

Yes.

> *She exits from the light and returns holding clothes.*
> *She goes to give them to him. He stares at her.*

ROSE

Do you need help getting these clothes on?

KOJI

Yes.

ROSE

Are you all right?

She begins to put his shirt on, arm by arm. She turns and begins to button up his shirt and then stops.

KOJI

I don't know. I want to be.

She touches him softly on the shoulder and then picks up a stray hair that lies on his shoulder. He places his hands on her face. They kiss, a long kiss.

ROSE and KOJI stand together in the space. The sound of an air-raid alarm broadcast over the radio. Throughout the following scenes, broadcasts from around the world rise in a collage that builds in accelerating frequency under the tension of the scenes.

FAT MAN gets up from the La-Z-Boy chair and stands dramatically at attention.

FAT MAN

I'm not sleeping! I'm ready. I wasn't ready but now I'm ready. That's right, I am a soldier despite myself. I am a living-room soldier. This country's backbone. The living-room soldier.

ROSE

Where does war start? Does it keep going until it ends in us and, when it does, where does it live?

KOJI

Where does it have to live to survive?

She opens his shirt and places her hand on his heart.

FAT MAN opens his shirt and pledges allegiance.

FAT MAN

I'm a soldier … I got a responsibility to uphold the fort no matter who the Indian is. I got to defend my country and my family.

He looks at ROUND ROSE and LITTLE BOY.

Even if my family are Indians.

He walks over and kisses them both on the head.

ROSE (*in Slavey and then in English*)

If I make you mine, then is everyone else the enemy?

KOJI

Kimi o watashi no mono ni shitara, tanin was minna teki ka?

He places his hand on her heart.

FAT MAN reaches under his La-Z-Boy chair and pulls out a wooden gun. He starts scouting around his living room.

FAT MAN pushes over his La-Z-Boy chair, setting up a barricade.

ROUND ROSE and LITTLE BOY hold each other's hand and stare at him.

ROSE

If you make me yours, do we make a world with no enemies?

FAT MAN

Just stand there. Nothing is wrong. I repeat, nothing is wrong. Everything is under control.

KOJI

Kimi ga watashi o jibun no mono ni shitara, teki-nashi no sekai ga dekiru no ka?

FAT MAN looks up as he listens to the air waves.

FAT MAN

I hear the enemy speaking and I know they are the enemy because they are speaking in a language I don't understand.

KOJI

If we make a world, we will make one where there are no enemies.

FAT MAN hears KOJI and looks suspiciously at ROUND ROSE and LITTLE BOY.

FAT MAN

I asked you people to just stand there and be quiet.

The sound of the intro to the Space Patrol *TV show from the 1950s. The TV flashes on and the face of the DENE SEER lights up and begins to buzz with a high Dene buzz.*

You hear that? You hear that? I knew it. It's not all in my mind. The aliens are here among us. Living like us but spying on us.

ROSE gets more afraid after each broadcast. KOJI touches her softly, comforting her in a lover's way.

LITTLE BOY begins to sing, his voice becoming louder and louder.

FAT MAN

Goddamnit! Who said you could sing! Who said you could sing! Shut that Indian up for Chrissakes, can't you see I'm trying to do something important here!

ROUND ROSE puts her hand on the boy.

ROSE

In the dark, I can hear it trying to come inside me like I am the radio. Like I am the radio and everything is coming through me and everything is getting bigger and louder until …

KOJI

Just hear me.

FAT MAN storms around the room, knocking over ROUND ROSE's collection of Japanese dolls.

FAT MAN

Who said you could put this shit in my house anyways? Christ! Pack this shit up and get it the hell out of my house; it's looking at me.

ROUND ROSE quietly moves around the living room, picking up her things and placing them softly in her suitcase. She begins to sing in Japanese under LITTLE BOY.

Shit, listen to them like they own the goddamn world. Well, I worked for this.

ROUND ROSE begins to take down a favourite piece.

Leave that. I like that.

ROUND ROSE backs away and stands by LITTLE BOY.

ROSE
The sound of it is getting right inside me, it's coming through the air like waves. I'm breathing it in. Oh God … make it stop.

KOJI
Look in me …

KOJI and ROSE shut their eyes, put their foreheads together, and begin to sing.

FAT MAN turns around and points a gun at LITTLE BOY and ROUND ROSE.

FAT MAN
I want you two aliens to get the hell out of my living room. You hear me? I said, I want you two ungrateful aliens to leave.

LITTLE BOY and ROUND ROSE stop and stare. Silence.

What don't you understand?

They begin to turn and grab their personal belongings.

Leave everything that is mine. And if you're in my house, it's mine.

ROSE

I can't take it anymore, I can't breathe anymore …

KOJI

Then breathe me in.

KOJI and ROSE sing into each other, merging their voices and bodies.

FAT MAN

Go back to where you came from.

Sound of a bomb going off in the desert.

FAT MAN reacts to the sound of bomb. He stares off to the sound. As he talks, ROUND ROSE and LITTLE BOY begin to leave. They join foreheads. ROUND ROSE helps him climb into the TV, into the Dene Seer. ROUND ROSE's shadow flares up and she walks into the shadow of TOKYO ROSE.

I think they are testing my neighbour … I think they got my neighbour. I said, I think they got my neighbour down the road. If they got my neighbour, I'm next, then you're next, that's how neighbourhoods work.

A warning sound and another bomb going off in the desert. FAT MAN swings around and sees that they are gone. He starts looking under things.

Where is my family? What did I say? I didn't mean you. I didn't mean it. I said it … I did it … but I didn't mean it!

Lights across the space begin to flicker on and off. FAT MAN sits down, shaken.

I'm sorry. What did I do wrong?

The small light of the pilothouse lights up blue to the voice of CAPTAIN MIKE.

CAPTAIN MIKE (*voiceover*)
Jesus Clist, I'm telling you to put your goddamn differences aside for one goddamn minute cuz we're all the same here in the nortd, we're all workin' togeder 'cause we all git to tink of our families and how'd hell we gonna feed dem. I'm sittin' in da pilothouse of dis goddamn … goddamn and all I wand to do is unload yor goddamn bullchit and open a bottle of rum under my goddamn pillow … and if I don't git my rum … And if we don't go farder than dis in dis goddamn century, we wont be goin' anywhere goddamn soon.

Complete darkness and then a radar light that circles the world. ROUND ROSE takes over.

ROUND ROSE
Hey neighbour … I'm sorry it's so … NOT Howdy Doody … Just kidding. Americans are Americans and everybody else is sorry. Half the time we don't even know what we are sorry about, it just squeaks out of our sorry gaps before we've even clued into the conversation. Well, I'm sorry YOU'RE all so sorry. You have to know when to be sorry. You can't really be sorry for something you don't want to remember, can you? Selective memory, isn't

it? Let's be honest, hell, you can't even apologize for the shit you did yesterday never mind fifty years ago. Indian residential schools, Japanese internment camps, hell, and this is just in your neighbourhood. But it's all right … everybody's sorry these days. The politicians are sorry, the cops are sorry, the priests are sorry, the logging companies are sorry, mining companies, electric companies, water companies, wife beaters, serial rapists, child molesters, mommy and daddy. Everybody's sorry. Everybody's sorry they got caught sticking it to someone else … that's what they are sorry about … getting caught. They could give a rat's ass about you, or me, or the people they are saying sorry to. Think about it ….Don't be a sorry ass, be sorry before you have to say you are sorry. Be sorry for even thinking about, bringing about something sorry-filled. And the next time someone says, "There is one law for everyone." Say, "I'm sorry, you're an idiot." Just kidding, now that was harsh. Any HOW, sayonara.

Lights out.

RADAR ECHOES

– Movement Four –

A precise instrument for seeing. The waves of radar getting closer to the heart of everything. The visions, the bombing, the burning.

The sound of worlds and hearts beating, truths colliding, and the tunnels of internal time digging deeper.

The high-frequency sound of radar, of the Dene Seer beginning to talk in Slavey.

LITTLE BOY emerges from the back of the TV. He embodies the Sahtu DENE SEER. His small body wears clothes that look too big for him. He walks in the light, his shadow projecting a tall elder as he eventually circles the space, retelling his story.

THE DENE SEER (*voiceover*)
After all this, after all this seer-singing, after this long night, I stopped singing. The vision finally complete. Finally silent. They spoke to me and asked me, "What is the matter? Did we do something wrong?"

*ROSE stands with her back to THE WIDOW. The
back of her dress is black. She kneads her bread on her
table. THE WIDOW yells from the fire.*

THE WIDOW

Why you standing way over there with your back turned?
Why don't you come closer so I can get a good Dene look
at you?

ROSE

How did you know I was here?

THE WIDOW

I could feel your back's eyes on me …

ROSE

I'll just be a minute if that's fine …

THE WIDOW

That's fine. Getting all stuck-up again. Making me wait.
Look at you, you think you were a miner with all that
black dust on you. How you get all that black rock on
you anyways?

ROSE

The wind's blowing it everywhere. The kids are playin' in
sandboxes of it, the caribou are eating it off the plants,
and we're drinkin' the water where they bury it. Besides
everybody's wearin' it these days, so I guess there's no
harm if a bit gets in my dough. It's as fine as flour anyways.

THE WIDOW

That's what they pay the scientists to say when the
government wants something.

ROSE

What's that?

THE WIDOW

There is no harm.

ROSE

What do you mean?

> *As THE WIDOW looks into the fire talking, ROSE turns around and walks toward her. She is eight months' pregnant, her clothes and face and arms are smudged with black, as is the loaf of bread she carries in her hands.*

THE WIDOW

The money rock will make anybody say anything so long as they can keep taking it out of our ground and, if everybody is making money, it doesn't matter about the people.

THE DENE SEER (*voiceover*)

They asked me, "Why did I sing all night? Why did I not let anyone rest?" I told them I sang many things and in the singing I saw the future, and I was disturbed.

> *THE WIDOW looks up at her belly and then at ROSE.*

ROSE

What are you talking about?

THE DENE SEER (*voiceover*)

In the singing, I felt they would hurt my people. My voice grew hoarse with the sight.

THE WIDOW

I'm just talking, that's all. Widows talk too much some
time. Too much time, I guess … You feelin' all right?

ROSE

I'm fine. Just fine.

THE WIDOW

Where's your baby's father?

ROSE

He's down the river fishing.

THE WIDOW

Indian? He looks sorta like an Indian but there's
something different going on.

ROSE

He's Indian enough from the other side.

THE WIDOW

I can't argue with that /

ROSE

/ Finally.

THE WIDOW

Not because I can't, but because I say you are like my
daughter.

THE DENE SEER (*voiceover*)

My voice grew hoarse with the sight of knowing that they
would harm my people from the inside.

*The light on THE MINER's hat goes on. He coughs
and coughs. Yellow spray comes from him as he
coughs.*

THE MINER

I'm sorry … did somebody say something? Do you wanna come closer? I'm not feeling so great so it'd be nice to talk to someone. There's too much that gets in a guy's mind when he's not feeling well and in the dark.

THE DENE SEER (*voiceover*)

I sang this strange vision of people going into a big hole in the ground – strange people, not Dene. Their skin was white. Strange. I followed.

He coughs hard.

THE MINER

Oh God, I feel it right here in my chest. I feel it right down inside me. I can feel it in my bones. It's damp here, and dark, and you can hear things, far away things …

THE DENE SEER (*voiceover*)

Inside. I followed them down. They were going into this dark hole in the earth with all kinds of metal tools and machines. All sorts of tools that made all sorts of noise deep inside.

THE MINER

And sometimes some of the guys say that being in here is like being in the womb again. But I sound too much like a woman saying that … and it's more like something's inside me, it's like something is inside me deep … making a lot of noise.

THE DENE SEER (*voiceover*)

I followed them knowing.

THE MINER

Why don't you come closer and sit down with me for a spell?

THE DENE SEER (*voiceover*)

They were digging great tunnels.

> *THE MINER coughs harder and harder … he bends over coughing.*

THE DENE SEER (*voiceover*)

On the surface where they came to live, they made strange houses. Strange houses with smoke coming out of them. Strange houses that looked the same for a people that all looked the same. Strange.

> *The sound of FAT MAN fumbling around in the dark. FAT MAN scrounges around in the dark and finally finds a flashlight. He flicks it on – nothing happens. He slams it – again, nothing …*

FAT MAN

Darkness courtesy of the goddamn bombs. Shit, nothing works anymore. They can build a goddamn atom bomb but they can't make batteries work when you need them. Assholes. I could really use that kid now. Fuck it. Just like a kid to take off when you really need him. Oh, it's okay, don't go feeling sorry for me. I just got matrimonial problems. I'm a happily married guy. Okay, I'm a married guy. She's a good girl. Quiet. She'll come back 'cause we got something real. She's not American but she is sorta. It just shows different cultures can get along if we're all willing to sit down and fuck … Talk. She's a good girl. A hard-working girl. She'll come back … you'll see.

THE DENE SEER (*voiceover*)
Strange.

The sound of an alarm.

FAT MAN
Excuse me.

He holds himself tighter and lies on the floor in a fetal position.

The sound of an explosion.

The flashlight pops on and flickers.

THE DENE SEER (*voiceover*)
I looked up inside my vision. I saw a flying bird, big. It landed and they loaded it with things. It didn't look like it could harm anybody, but it made a lot of noise. I watched them digging something out of the hole in the earth and I watched them raise it to the cool sky until it disappeared and reappeared. Burning.

An older, middle-aged, very Japanese ROUND ROSE sits passively at a mike in the storeroom of her father's Japanese souvenir store. She sits among the souvenirs as she broadcasts.

ROUND ROSE
Greetings … I have a job working in my father's store. Not as glamorous as my life once was. Not as young. I have aged while stocking Japanese gifts on shelves in my father's Japanese-American store. Keeping my hands busy, dreaming of the past. You do not recognize me? Why should you, I do not recognize me. My hope has

aged. Can I give you a little farewell gift, a souvenir? It is no trouble. No trouble. See. See this white notepaper.

She takes a piece of white notepaper and folds a crane.

ROUND ROSE
Let me fold it with old patient hands, here, here, I am transforming my reality into a beautiful bird. No, I am not bitter. I am not. No. I am not bitter. I am disappointed. My notepaper of hope is a disappointed white bird.

The sound of one pair of very loud footsteps. LABINE BROTHER ONE, holding a Geiger counter to the earth, walks around the circle of ghostly images.

The sound of the Geiger counter clicking.

The following scene starts out slow and begins to escalate in fear as characters and worlds collide.

LABINE BROTHER ONE
We opened it up and it's still here. Hear it? Uranium. There's no telling what the sound of money is until you actually hear it. You never forget that sound and it never forgets you. Listen to this. Click … click … click …

THE RADIUM PAINTER clicks in wearing a hospital gown. She begins to place radium-painted clocks in a circle as they all begin to tick loudly.

The sound of a heart beating.

ROSE
Listen to this … He's got a strong heartbeat. I think he's a boy.

She talks to her baby.

My name's Rose ... and I was gonna call you Rose, like my mother and my mother's mother but I guess if you're a boy you should get a tougher name ... like Thorn. Just kidding. Listen ... beat ... beat ... beat ...

She begins to walk in the circle.

The sound of the Geiger counter.

LABINE BROTHER ONE

Jesus, what a beautiful sound ... click ... click ... click ... As if they could send a bunch of so-called "experts" up here and convince me that this uranium is like a goddamn grenade going off.

The sound of clocks.

THE RADIUM PAINTER stops and begins to undress. Taking a white wedding dress from a uranium sack, she holds it desperately.

THE RADIUM PAINTER

My name is ... Frances ... and I'm going to paint the clocks slower.

The sound of THE MINER coughing.

THE MINER

Is that you, darlin'? It's me. I've been waiting long enough. I want to see you now. Are you ready?

The sound of clocks. She talks to them.

THE RADIUM PAINTER

My name is Frances. Frances … tick … tick … tick …
Time can be ugly but your face is beautiful. I made you
beautiful and what will you do for me? Could you slow
down for me … tick … tick … tick. Take it slow … like
I'll say to my miner on my wedding night.

The sound of THE MINER coughing.

THE MINER

Don't be scared, Frances … it's just me … you got to
remember who I am. I'm the man who loves you.

THE RADIUM PAINTER

Tick … tick … tick … Slow down, lover. Slow down for
me … slow down for me.

The sound of the Geiger counter clicking aggressively.

LABINE BROTHER ONE

These goddamn assholes say they got proof that other
uranium miners in Europe are dead from cancers, that
those radium painters died of cancers. That uranium is
like shrapnel … click … click … click. Like deadly
particles of energy that never die.

ROSE

The widow worries all the time now. She says she's
worried about the word "cancer." She says she's worried
for the men who carried it for them … carried it the /

LABINE BROTHER ONE

/ The particles just keep embedding and decaying
everything that's touched them. I say, "Just think of the
money" /

THE RADIUM PAINTER
/ Tick … tick … tick … /

LABINE BROTHER ONE
/ Click … click … click.

THE MINER
Oh Frances, you are like a beautiful vision. My vision.

The sound of the Geiger counter clicking.

LABINE BROTHER ONE
Radioactive? Doesn't sound like such a bad word to me.

ROSE
The widow says there is no word in Dene for radioactive.

The sound of clocks ticking.

THE RADIUM PAINTER
Tick … tick … tick … Slow down … please slow down.

The sound of THE MINER coughing.

THE MINER
Oh, you are so beautiful. So beautiful.

The sound of clocks ticking.

THE RADIUM PAINTER
Just stay there for a minute … tick … tick … tick …
watches … compasses … tick … tick … tick … time to
love … time to have babies … time to tell you …

The sound of a baby's heartbeat.

ROSE
I have hope inside me. It lives inside me. Here. See. Can
you hear? Beat … beat … beat.

THE MINER gets closer to THE RADIUM PAINTER and continues coughing.

THE MINER
Ahh … honey, it's all right. Whatever it is, it's all right.

ROSE
Beat … / beat … beat /

THE RADIUM PAINTER
/ I had a dream we would get married and we could move the furniture aside in our living room and dance like married couples do in the movies /

THE MINER stops.

ROSE
/ Beat … beat … beat.

THE MINER
A married couple. You and me.

FAT MAN alone in his living room, pacing around.

The sound of radar beeps getting closer.

FAT MAN
Maybe I should have expected more from myself. I mean, there's got to be more than having a dead-end job and living this ass-covering rhetoric. I feel like a complete asshole. A complete dummy now … You know what I mean?

THE RADIUM PAINTER
I wanted more. I wanted to live.

FAT MAN

    Do you know what I mean?

THE RADIUM PAINTER

    I wanted to dream small, living dreams.

    She begins to cry.

LABINE BROTHER ONE

    Christ, these crybaby "experts" say it's dangerous to even
    breathe a few little particles in, never mind handling it,
    but … what does anybody really know.

ROSE

    I have hope for the world no matter what anybody says /

THE RADIUM PAINTER

    / Tick … tick … tick.

    The sound of the Geiger counter clicking loudly.

THE MINER

    Why don't you put your wedding dress on? You'll feel
    better if you put it on. Darlin'?

    The sound of a heartbeat.

ROSE

    My baby's going to be mixed again, but I'm happy about
    that 'cause I think he can give the world my hope. Listen.
    Beat … beat … beat …

    The sound of beeping as a radar target gets closer.

    *THE RADIUM PAINTER stands slowly with her
    back to him and begins to put on her dress.*

FAT MAN

I've been lying here ass-up to the world, in a house that is not a home, in a makeshift world where nothing is real. I've been bending over while they bomb the shit out of my neighbourhood.

> *The sound of the Geiger counter gets louder and louder.*

ROSE

His heart is so strong you have to believe in the world.

LABINE BROTHER ONE

Christ, how many discoverers have to listen to this bullshit. I'm trying to run a corporation here. I'm trying to keep men employed so they can feed their families.

ROSE

You have to believe in the future no matter what.

THE MINER

Frances? Turn around now. Please. Oh God, Frances /

THE RADIUM PAINTER

/ Beat … beat … beat … /

ROSE

/ Tick … tick … tick.

> *FAT MAN screams over at LABINE BROTHER ONE.*

FAT MAN

This is my neighbourhood, you hear me … you … you … liar.

LABINE BROTHER ONE

… The hell with you, and the HELL with them. The government knows what it's doing and the government is behind me /

FAT MAN

/ I might be a complete fuckin' dummy just about to die /

LABINE BROTHER ONE

/ and I'm behind them /

FAT MAN

/ just about to die but I know liars. You are all a pack of goddamn liars!

The sound of the Geiger counter clicking.

LABINE BROTHER ONE

We talk the same liar language. I mean, we understand how things are done in the new world. The real world.

THE MINER gets closer to THE RADIUM PAINTER.

THE RADIUM PAINTER

I'm sorry. I'm sorry.

ROSE

You have to start when they are young and their hearts are strong.

THE MINER

Everything's gonna be all right. Everything is fine, you'll see.

He grabs her hand from behind. She takes it.

ROSE

You have to believe that the world is a beautiful place.

THE MINER pulls her hand tenderly and turns her around in her wedding dress. THE RADIUM PAINTER turns around. Half her face is missing and her beautiful hair is entirely gone.

THE MINER

Ah … Jesus … Sweet Jesus … Who did this to you? Ahhh …

He sinks in horror and finally curls down and cries.

The sound of the Geiger counter gets closer.

THE RADIUM PAINTER

Tick … tick … tick

The sound of radar beeping closer and closer.

ROSE cradles her belly in protection.

ROSE

It's okay, baby, I'll protect you. I look delicate but I'm strong.

The sound of footsteps gets louder and scarier. The sound of the Geiger counter approaches very loudly …

THE RADIUM PAINTER draws closer to THE MINER. She holds her hand to him. He doesn't look up but takes her hand as she helps pull him up. They begin to dance.

THE MINER

I'm sorry … I'm so sick … I'm so sorry. Why did they do this to you … us … I'm … oh … / God, help us … help us … /

THE RADIUM PAINTER holds him and they waltz slowly.

THE RADIUM PAINTER

/ Slow down, lover.

The sound of radar close and loud.

FAT MAN sits down in his La-Z-Boy chair and cries.

The sound of footsteps and the sound of the Geiger counter get louder and louder, closer and closer.

FAT MAN

I'm sorry. Did you hear me? God, it's so simple, I want you to just hold my hand. I don't even want a job. I don't want to die alone. I'm sorry.

From the darkness of his living-room barricade. ROUND ROSE leans into his light and grabs his hand.

ROUND ROSE

I forgive you. I am here.

The sound of the Geiger counter gets closer and closer and it is now louder than it's ever been as it clicks toward ROSE, circling in on her.

LABINE BROTHER ONE looks in horror as the Geiger counter hits her belly …

The sound of a bomb falling as LABINE BROTHER ONE looks at ROSE and then directly at her belly.

LABINE BROTHER ONE
I didn't know.

ROSE looks at her belly and up to the sky in horror.

ROSE
Mother, make it lighter ... sing, pleasssssssssssssse.

The sound of the bomb falls downward and into their bodies that glow bright and then ...

They all look up ...

The sound of an explosion.

A huge light whites out their world into blackness.

U.S. DEFENSE WAR PROPAGANDA CLIP
"The most beautiful thing in the history of mankind."

A black dust has settled over everything.

Lights up on FAT MAN's living room where a sack-dummy sits in its chair, worse for wear. On the couch, a sack-dummy that looks like ROUND ROSE sits, holding the hand of the sack-dummy FAT MAN.

THE DENE SEER (*voiceover*)
I wondered if this would happen on our land, or if it would harm our people.

The sound of Japanese drums.

*Total quiet. The sound of a faint heartbeat as THE
JAPANESE GRANDMOTHER makes her way across
the blackened land, through small notepapers of
folded cranes, through charred bodies and small fires,
through the turning steps of THE RADIUM
PAINTER, the bride-to-be. THE JAPANESE
GRANDMOTHER marches beautifully through
everything in a traditional red kimono toward the
burnt cherry tree.*

The people they dropped this burning on … looked like
us, like Dene.

*THE JAPANESE GRANDMOTHER gets close to the
blackened body of KOJI as he lies at the base of the
burnt cherry tree. KOJI's hand lies outstretched
holding her note, his other hand reaching toward the
branch. She takes the note from his hands and, crying,
begins to read it in Japanese.*

THE JAPANESE GRANDMOTHER
"If we ever get separated, you are to wait for me here.
Wait for me here and I will come for you. Remember this
tree, remember my words."

*THE JAPANESE GRANDMOTHER takes off her
long red kimono and tucks in her grandson. She turns
and becomes THE WIDOW. She takes off her scarf
and lets her long hair flow. She kneels to the ground
and from her fire gathers the blackened body of her
beautiful young husband.*

THE DENE SEER (*voiceover*)

This burning vision is not for us now … it will come a long time in the future. It will come burning inside.

THE WIDOW

So many fires now, so many fires still burning. I've looked through this fire over time like a dream loving you long. Here, here is the jacket I beaded for you, your caribou-hide jacket that smells of a time when we were just a man and a woman. It smells good.

He reaches up to her. She begins to put his jacket on his body.

You have carried our burden long enough; you do not have to carry me. I will carry you inside. I will still say I love you out loud. I will still wait for you. I will still wait for you to come home … till I die.

Released, her husband begins to walk toward the fire shadows of waiting DENE ORE CARRIERS. He disappears into the spirit world. An ember remains in the fire. She looks at the fire as it goes out. Time passes. KOJI, her grown grandson, puts his hand on her shoulder.

KOJI THE GRANDSON

Grandma. It's time to go. No more now, Mom wouldn't want to see you like this.

THE WIDOW

She made beautiful bread. Did I tell you she used to bring me bread? It tasted good too. I miss her.

KOJI THE GRANDSON

Come now, you are like my mother. You grew me to be
a man.

THE WIDOW

They used to pay a dollar for it. That was a lot of money
in those days.

KOJI THE GRANDSON

I know, Grandma.

THE WIDOW

You look like her. You look like him. You are my special
grandson. My small man now. My small man that
survived. Tough like hope. If we listen, we can hear them
too.

KOJI THE GRANDSON

I know Obachan. I know. I can hear them. They hear us.

*The sound of the radio dial gliding over voices that
are calling their loved ones home.*

SLAVEY ANNOUNCER (*voiceover*)

Na-aa-solt-nen-agan, mussi-naga-gwhat-ta, quau-na-
nagot-ta-na-lay, atay-swey,sa-la-do-ay, r-yonay,
neeaownet-u, naga-whata-mussi-mussi.

*The sound of the radio dial gliding over Japanese
voices that are calling their loved ones home.*

JAPANESE ANNOUNCER (*voiceover*)

Kon-nichi-wa Oji-chan, ankiki, ne-san, musuko, otosan,
aibo, sensei, wagako, koibito yo. Sabishii kara hayaku
kaette koi!

The sound of the radio dial gliding over Canadian voices that are calling their loved ones home.

CANADIAN ANNOUNCER (*voiceover*)
Hello, Granddad, brother, sister, son, husband, father, cousin, nephew, friend, my teacher, my love … We love you and miss you.

The cherry blossoms fall.

THE WIDOW and KOJI THE GRANDSON stand and look up and listen.

KOJI THE GRANDSON
They hear us, and they are talking back in hope over time.

Glowing herds of caribou move in unison over the vast empty landscape as cherry blossoms fall until they fill the stage.

Marie Clements is an award-winning performer, writer, director, producer, and co-director of red diva projects and frog girl films. As a writer, Marie's work has garnered numerous productions, publications, and awards, including the 2004 Canada-Japan Literary Award for *Burning Vision* and two shortlisted nominations for the Governor General's Award for Drama, in 2004 for *Burning Vision* and in 2008 for *Copper Thunderbird*. Marie has worked extensively in and across a variety of mediums, including theatre, performance, film, new media, radio, and television.